Waves and Information Technologies

elevatescience
MODULES

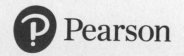 **Pearson**

Boston, Massachusetts **Chandler, Arizona**
Glenview, Illinois **New York, New York**

AUTHORS

You're an author!

As you write in this science book, your answers and personal discoveries will be recorded for you to keep, making this book unique to you. That is why you are one of the primary authors of this book.

✏️ **In the space below, print your name, school, town, and state. Then write a short autobiography that includes your interests and accomplishments.**

YOUR NAME ....

SCHOOL ....

TOWN, STATE ....

AUTOBIOGRAPHY ....

....

....

....

....

Your Photo

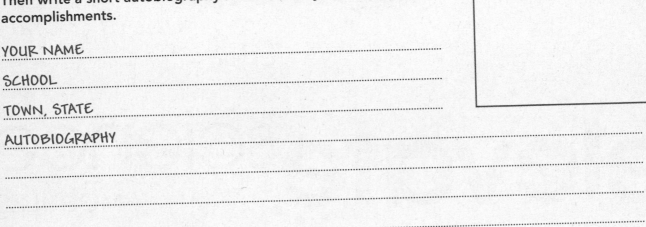

Pearson Education, Inc. 330 Hudson Street, New York, NY 10013

Next Generation Science Standards is a registered trademark of Achieve. Neither Achieve nor the lead states and partners that developed the Next Generation Science Standards were involved in the production of this product, and do not endorse it. NGSS Lead States. 2013. *Next Generation Science Standards: For States, By States.* Washington, DC: The National Academies Press.

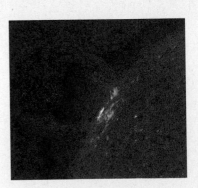

The cover photo shows a close-up of a solar flare.

Front cover: Solar Flare, Stocktrek Images, Inc./Alamy Stock Photo; Back cover: Science Doodle, LHF Graphics/ Shutterstock.

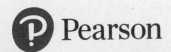 **Pearson**

ISBN-13: 978-1-418-29155-6
ISBN-10: 1-418-29155-2
2   18

Program Authors

ZIPPORAH MILLER, EdD

Coordinator for K-12 Science Programs, Anne Arundel County Public Schools
Dr. Zipporah Miller currently serves as the Senior Manager for Organizational Learning with the Anne Arundel County Public School System. Prior to that she served as the K-12 Coordinator for science in Anne Arundel County. She conducts national training to science stakeholders on the Next Generation Science Standards. Dr. Miller also served as the Associate Executive Director for Professional Development Programs and conferences at the National Science Teachers Association (NSTA) and served as a reviewer during the development of Next Generation Science Standards. Dr. Miller holds a doctoral degree from the University of Maryland College Park, a master's degree in school administration and supervision from Bowie State University and a bachelor's degree from Chadron State College.

MICHAEL J. PADILLA, PhD

Professor Emeritus, Eugene P. Moore School of Education, Clemson University, Clemson, South Carolina
Michael J. Padilla taught science in middle and secondary schools, has more than 30 years of experience educating middle-school science teachers, and served as one of the writers of the 1996 U.S. National Science Education Standards. In recent years Mike has focused on teaching science to English Language Learners. His extensive experience as Principal Investigator on numerous National Science Foundation and U.S. Department of Education grants resulted in more than $35 million in funding to improve science education. He served as president of the National Science Teachers Association, the world's largest science teaching organization, in 2005–6.

MICHAEL E. WYSESSION, PhD

Professor of Earth and Planetary Sciences, Washington University, St. Louis, Missouri
Author of more than 100 science and science education publications, Dr. Wysession was awarded the prestigious National Science Foundation Presidential Faculty Fellowship and Packard Foundation Fellowship for his research in geophysics, primarily focused on using seismic tomography to determine the forces driving plate tectonics. Dr. Wysession is also a leader in geoscience literacy and education; he is the chair of the Earth Science Literacy Initiative, the author of several popular video lectures on geology in the *Great Courses* series, and a lead writer of the *Next Generation Science Standards**.

REVIEWERS

Program Consultants

Carol Baker
Science Curriculum

Dr. Carol K. Baker is superintendent for Lyons Elementary K-8 School District in Lyons, Illinois. Prior to this, she was Director of Curriculum for Science and Music in Oak Lawn, Illinois. Before this she taught Physics and Earth Science for 18 years. In the recent past, Dr. Baker also wrote assessment questions for ACT (EXPLORE and PLAN), was elected president of the Illinois Science Teachers Association from 2011–2013, and served as a member of the Museum of Science and Industry (Chicago) advisory board. She is a writer of the Next Generation Science Standards. Dr. Baker received her B.S. in Physics and a science teaching certification. She completed her master's of Educational Administration (K-12) and earned her doctorate in Educational Leadership.

Jim Cummins
ELL

Dr. Cummins's research focuses on literacy development in multilingual schools and the role technology plays in learning across the curriculum. *Elevate Science* incorporates research-based principles for integrating language with the teaching of academic content based on Dr. Cummins's work.

Elfrieda Hiebert
Literacy

Dr. Hiebert, a former primary-school teacher, is President and CEO of TextProject, a non-profit aimed at providing open-access resources for instruction of beginning and struggling readers, She is also a research associate at the University of California Santa Cruz. Her research addresses how fluency, vocabulary, and knowledge can be fostered through appropriate texts, and her contributions have been recognized through awards such as the Oscar Causey Award for Outstanding Contributions to Reading Research (Literacy Research Association, 2015), Research to Practice award (American Educational Research Association, 2013), and the William S. Gray Citation of Merit Award for Outstanding Contributions to Reading Research (International Reading Association, 2008).

Content Reviewers

Alex Blom, Ph.D.
Associate Professor
Department Of Physical Sciences
Alverno College
Milwaukee, Wisconsin

Joy Branlund, Ph.D.
Department of Physical Science
Southwestern Illinois College
Granite City, Illinois

Judy Calhoun
Associate Professor
Physical Sciences
Alverno College
Milwaukee, Wisconsin

Stefan Debbert
Associate Professor of Chemistry
Lawrence University
Appleton, Wisconsin

Diane Doser
Professor
Department of Geological Sciences
University of Texas at El Paso
El Paso, Texas

Rick Duhrkopf, Ph.D.
Department of Biology
Baylor University
Waco, Texas

Jennifer Liang
University of Minnesota Duluth
Duluth, Minnesota

Heather Mernitz, Ph.D.
Associate Professor of Physical Sciences
Alverno College
Milwaukee, Wisconsin

Joseph McCullough, Ph.D.
Cabrillo College
Aptos, California

Katie M. Nemeth, Ph.D.
Assistant Professor
College of Science and Engineering
University of Minnesota Duluth
Duluth, Minnesota

Maik Pertermann
Department of Geology
Western Wyoming Community College
Rock Springs, Wyoming

Scott Rochette
Department of the Earth Sciences
The College at Brockport
State University of New York
Brockport, New York

David Schuster
Washington University in St Louis
St. Louis, Missouri

Shannon Stevenson
Department of Biology
University of Minnesota Duluth
Duluth, Minnesota

Paul Stoddard, Ph.D.
Department of Geology and Environmental Geosciences
Northern Illinois University
DeKalb, Illinois

Nancy Taylor
American Public University
Charles Town, West Virginia

Teacher Reviewers

Jennifer Bennett, M.A.
Memorial Middle School
Tampa, Florida

Sonia Blackstone
Lake County Schools
Howey In the Hills, Florida

Teresa Bode
Roosevelt Elementary
Tampa, Florida

Tyler C. Britt, Ed.S.
Curriculum & Instructional
 Practice Coordinator
Raytown Quality Schools
Raytown, Missouri

A. Colleen Campos
Grandview High School
Aurora, Colorado

Ronald Davis
Riverview Elementary
Riverview, Florida

Coleen Doulk
Challenger School
Spring Hill, Florida

Mary D. Dube
Burnett Middle School
Seffner, Florida

Sandra Galpin
Adams Middle School
Tampa, Florida

Margaret Henry
Lebanon Junior High School
Lebanon, Ohio

Christina Hill
Beth Shields Middle School
Ruskin, Florida

Judy Johnis
Gorden Burnett Middle School
Seffner, Florida

Karen Y. Johnson
Beth Shields Middle School
Ruskin, Florida

Jane Kemp
Lockhart Elementary School
Tampa, Florida

Denise Kuhling
Adams Middle School
Tampa, Florida

Esther Leonard, M.Ed. and L.M.T.
Gifted and talented Implementation Specialist
San Antonio Independent School District
San Antonio, Texas

Kelly Maharaj
Challenger K–8 School of Science
 and Mathematics
Spring Hill, Florida

Kevin J. Maser, Ed.D.
H. Frank Carey Jr/Sr High School
Franklin Square, New York

Angie L. Matamoros, Ph.D.
ALM Science Consultant
Weston, Florida

Corey Mayle
Brogden Middle School
Durham, North Carolina

Keith McCarthy
George Washington Middle School
Wayne, New Jersey

Yolanda O. Peña
John F. Kennedy Junior High School
West Valley City, Utah

Kathleen M. Poe
Jacksonville Beach Elementary School
Jacksonville Beach, Florida

Wendy Rauld
Monroe Middle School
Tampa, Florida

Anne Rice
Woodland Middle School
Gurnee, Illinois

Bryna Selig
Gaithersburg Middle School
Gaithersburg, Maryland

Pat (Patricia) Shane, Ph.D.
STEM & ELA Education Consultant
Chapel Hill, North Carolina

Diana Shelton
Burnett Middle School
Seffner, Florida

Nakia Sturrup
Jennings Middle School
Seffner, Florida

Melissa Triebwasser
Walden Lake Elementary
Plant City, Florida

Michele Bubley Wiehagen
Science Coach
Miles Elementary School
Tampa, Florida

Pauline Wilcox
Instructional Science Coach
Fox Chapel Middle School
Spring Hill, Florida

Safety Reviewers

Douglas Mandt, M.S.
Science Education Consultant
Edgewood, Washington

Juliana Textley, Ph.D.
Author, NSTA books on school science safety
Adjunct Professor
Lesley University
Cambridge, Massachusetts

TOPIC 1
Waves and Electromagnetic Radiation

.... x

The Essential Question What are the properties of mechanical and electromagnetic waves?

Quest KICKOFF Design to Stop a Thief

.... 2

MS-PS4-1, MS-PS4-2

LESSON 1 Wave Properties 4
  Literacy Connection Integrate Information 7
  Math Toolbox Use Proportional Relationships 10
  Quest CHECK-IN Light Behavior 11
  Case Study Sound and Light at the Ballpark 12

LESSON 2 Wave Interactions 14
  Literacy Connection Integrate Information 17
  Quest CHECK-IN Virtual Optics 22
  uEngineer It! STEM Say "Cheese!" 23

LESSON 3 Sound Waves 24
  Math Toolbox Reason Quantitatively 30
  Literacy Connection Integrate with Visuals 32

LESSON 4 Electromagnetic Waves 34
  Literacy Connection Translate Information 38
  Math Toolbox Draw Comparative Inferences 39
  Quest CHECK-INS Optical Demonstration 42
  Career Lighting Designer 43

LESSON 5 Light 44
  Literacy Connection Evaluate Media 47
  Quest CHECK-IN An Optimum Optical Solution 53

Review and Assess 54
  Evidence-Based Assessment 56
  Quest FINDINGS Reflect on Your Demonstration 57
  uDemonstrate Making Waves 58

Go to PearsonRealize.com to access your digital course.

▶ **VIDEO**
- Lighting Designer

👆 **INTERACTIVITY**
- Modeling Waves
- Making Waves
- Describe the Properties of Waves
- Model Wave Interactions
- Use Models to Describe Wave Behavior
- Reflection, Transmission, and Absorption of Sound Waves
- Sound
- Doppler Effect
- Build an Electromagnetic Wave
- Models of Light
- Describe Electromagnetic Waves
- Describe the Behavior of Light
- Blinded by the Light
- Predict the Behavior of Light Rays

📱 **VIRTUAL LAB**

☑ **ASSESSMENT**

📖 **eTEXT**

📱 **APP**

HANDS-ON LABS

uConnect What Are Waves?

uInvestigate
- Waves and Their Characteristics
- Wave Behavior
- Understanding Sound
- Build a Wave
- Light Interacting with Matter

uDemonstrate
Making Waves

TOPIC
2
Information Technologies 62

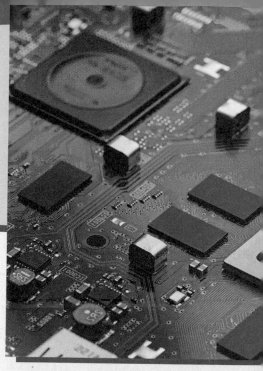

The Essential Question Why are digital signals a reliable way to produce, store, and transmit information?

Quest KICKOFF Testing, Testing . . . 1, 2, 3 64

MS-PS4-3

LESSON 1 Electric Circuits 66
   Literacy Connection Determine Central Ideas 68
   Math Toolbox Use Proportional Relationships 70
   Quest CHECK-IN Constructing a Microphone 74
   иEngineer It! STEM A Life-Saving Mistake 75

LESSON 2 Signals 76
   Literacy Connection Summarize Texts 80
   Math Toolbox Draw Comparative Inferences 82
   Quest CHECK-IN Analog and Digital Recordings 85
   Case Study Super Ultra High Definition! 86

LESSON 3 Communication and Technology 88
   Literacy Connection Cite Textual Evidence 90
   Math Toolbox Analyze Relationships 91
   Quest CHECK-IN Evaluate Recording Technologies 96
   Extraordinary Science Beam Me Up! 97

Review and Assess 98
   Evidence-Based Assessment 100
   Quest FINDINGS Reflect on Your Recording Method 101
   иDemonstrate Over and Out 102

Science and Engineering Practices Handbook 106
Appendices, Glossary, Index 118

Go to PearsonRealize.com to access your digital course.

▶ **VIDEO**
• Network Administrator

👆 **INTERACTIVITY**
• Electric Circuits
• How Can You Light the Lights?
• Analog and Digital Signals
• I've Got to Take This Call
• Digitized Images
• Film Cameras and Digital Cameras
• Technology and Communication
• Signal Reliability

📱 **VIRTUAL LAB**

☑ **ASSESSMENT**

📖 **eTEXT**

📱 **APP**

HANDS-ON LABS

иConnect Continuous or Discrete?

иInvestigate
• Electric Current and Voltage
• Constructing a Simple Computer Circuit
• Let the Music Play

иDemonstrate
Over and Out

Elevate your thinking!

Elevate Science takes science to a whole new level and lets you take ownership of your learning. Explore science in the world around you. Investigate how things work. Think critically and solve problems! *Elevate Science* helps you think like a scientist, so you're ready for a world of discoveries.

Explore Your World

Explore real-life scenarios with engaging Quests that dig into science topics around the world. You can:

- Solve real-world problems
- Apply skills and knowledge
- Communicate solutions

Make Connections

Elevate Science connects science to other subjects and shows you how to better understand the world through:

- Mathematics
- Reading and Writing
- Literacy

Quest KICKOFF

What do you think is causing Pleasant Pond to turn green?

In 2016, algal blooms turned bodies of water green and slimy in Florida, Utah, California, and 17 other states. These blooms put people and ecosystems in danger. Scientists, such as limnologists, are working to predict and prevent future algal blooms. In this problem-based Quest activity, you will investigate an algal bloom at a lake and determine its cause. In labs and digital activities, you will apply what you learn in each lesson to help you gather evidence to solve the mystery. With enough evidence, you will be able to identify what you believe is the cause of the algal bloom and present a solution in the Findings activity.

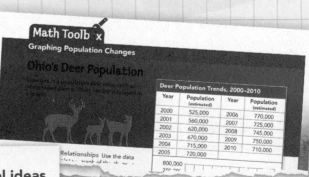

Math Toolbox
Graphing Population Changes

Ohio's Deer Population

Changes in a population over time, such as Ohio's deer population over a decade, can be displayed in a graph.

Deer Population Trends, 2000–2010

Year	Population (estimated)	Year	Population (estimated)
2000	525,000	2006	770,000
2001	560,000	2007	725,000
2002	620,000	2008	745,000
2003	670,000	2009	750,000
2004	715,000	2010	710,000
2005	720,000		

Relationships Use the data

800,000
750,000

READING CHECK   Determine Central ideas
What adaptations might the giraffe have that help it survive in its environment?

Academic Vocabulary
Relate the term *decomposer* to the verb *compose*. What does it mean to compose something?

Build Skills for the Future

- Master the Engineering Design Process
- Apply critical thinking and analytical skills
- Learn about STEM careers

Focus on Inquiry

Case studies put you in the shoes of a scientist to solve real-world mysteries using real data. You will be able to:

- Analyze Data
- Test a hypothesis
- Solve the Case

Case Study

MS-LS2-1

THE CASE OF THE DISAPPEARING

Cerulean Warbler

The cerulean warbler is a small, migratory songbird named for its blue color. Cerulean warblers breed in eastern North America during the spring and summer. The warblers spend the winter months in the Andes Mountains of Colombia, Venezuela, Ecuador, and Peru in northern part of South America.

Enter the Lab

Hands-on experiments and virtual labs help you test ideas and show what you know in performance-based assessments. Scaffolded labs include:

- STEM Labs
- Design Your Own
- Open-ended Labs

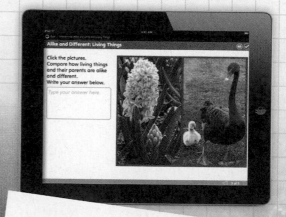

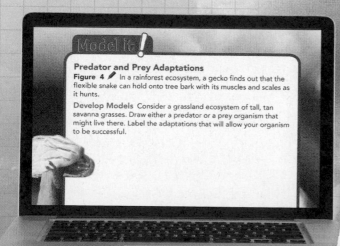

Predator and Prey Adaptations

Figure 4 In a rainforest ecosystem, a gecko finds out that the flexible snake can hold onto tree bark with its muscles and scales as it hunts.

Develop Models Consider a grassland ecosystem of tall, tan savanna grasses. Draw either a predator or a prey organism that might live there. Label the adaptations that will allow your organism to be successful.

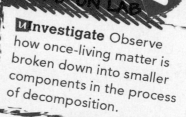

HANDS-ON LAB

Investigate Observe how once-living matter is broken down into smaller components in the process of decomposition.

Waves and Electromagnetic Radiation

LESSON 1
Wave Properties

uInvestigate Lab: Waves and Their Characteristics

LESSON 2
Wave Interactions

uInvestigate Lab: Wave Behavior

uEngineer It! STEM **Say "Cheese"!**

LESSON 3
Sound Waves

uInvestigate Lab: Understanding Sound

LESSON 4
Electromagnetic Waves

uInvestigate Lab: Build a Wave

LESSON 5
Light

uInvestigate Lab: Light Interacting With Matter

NGSS PERFORMANCE EXPECTATIONS

MS-PS4-1 Use mathematical representations to describe a simple model for waves that includes how the amplitude of a wave is related to the energy in a wave.

MS-PS4-2 Develop and use a model to describe that waves are reflected, absorbed, or transmitted through various materials.

HANDS-ON LAB

uConnect See how particles on a wave move in this rope experiment.

GO ONLINE
to access your
digital course

▶ VIDEO

👆 INTERACTIVITY

🧪 VIRTUAL LAB

☑ ASSESSMENT

📖 eTEXT

⚗ HANDS-ON LABS

How are these laser beams made?

The Essential Question

What are the properties of mechanical and electromagnetic waves?

The boats in this harbor bob gently up and down due to the motion of water waves. But the laser light show is also made of waves—light waves! What do you think these two types of waves have in common?

....

....

....

....

1

Quest KICKOFF

How can you design a system to stop a thief?

NBC LEARN ▶ VIDEO

STEM ▶ **Phenomenon** It may seem like something out of the movies, but some security systems use lasers to help prevent the theft of priceless objects. Engineers apply their knowledge of light and how it behaves to design these security systems. In this Quest activity, you will explore how light waves interact with lenses and mirrors. You will design possible solutions for a security demonstration and then test and evaluate your solutions to determine the optimal design. After making any additional modifications, you will demonstrate your expertise by directing a beam of light around an obstacle to reach

After watching the Quest Kickoff video, think about a problem in your community that might be solved with the use of lasers. Record your solutions. Then share your ideas with a partner and discuss how lasers are important to our daily lives.

....

....

....

....

....

....

....

....

....

MS-PS4-1 Use mathematical representations to describe a simple model for waves that includes how the amplitude of a wave is related to the energy in a wave.
MS-PS4-2 Develop and use a model to describe that waves are reflected, absorbed, or transmitted through various materials.

👆 **INTERACTIVITY**

Design to Stop a Thief

Quest CHECK-IN

IN LESSON 1
What effects do lenses and mirrors have on a beam of light? Explore models to observe how light interacts with different objects.

👆 **INTERACTIVITY**

Light Behavior

Quest CHECK-IN

IN LESSON 2
What happens when light waves are reflected or transmitted? Experiment with mirrors and lenses to observe how they affect light waves.

👆 **INTERACTIVITY**

Virtual Optics

IN LESSON 3
How do the properties of sound waves differ from light waves? Consider the properties of waves in your solution.

Museums use high-tech security systems to protect priceless works of art.

Quest CHECK-IN

IN LESSON 4

How can you make a beam of light bend around an object? Develop and evaluate possible solutions to the challenge.

INTERACTIVITY

Optical Demonstration

Quest CHECK-IN

IN LESSON 5

STEM How can you apply your knowledge of lenses and mirrors to your solution? Build and test a solution, using lenses and mirrors. Then communicate your solution in a presentation or visual display.

HANDS-ON LAB

An Optimal Optical Solution

Quest FINDINGS

Complete the Quest!

Evaluate your security system designs and reflect on the design and engineering process.

INTERACTIVITY

Reflect on Your Demonstration

3

Wave Properties

Guiding Questions

- How can you use a simple model to describe a wave and its features?
- How can you observe the properties of waves?
- What kinds of patterns can you predict based on wave properties?

Connections

Literacy Integrate Information

Math Use Proportional Relationships

MS-PS4-1

HANDS-ON LAB

uInvestigate Model the three different types of mechanical waves.

Vocabulary

wave
mechanical wave
medium
electromagnetic
 radiation
transverse wave
amplitude
longitudinal wave
wavelength
frequency

Academic Vocabulary

vacuum

Connect It !

✏ **Read the caption, and then label the photos with different types of waves that are indicated in some way by the photos.**

Engage in Argument How is Earth dependent on the sun for energy?

....

....

....

Connect to Society How is a tsunami warning system a benefit to society?

....

....

Types of Waves

When you think of a wave, you probably picture a surface wave on the ocean. Actually, a **wave** is any disturbance that transfers energy from place to place. An ocean wave is one type of wave called a **mechanical wave**, meaning it moves through some type of matter. The matter a wave travels through is called a **medium**. A mechanical wave cannot travel through a **vacuum**, such as space.

Sound waves are another type of mechanical wave. Sound can travel through the ocean, but it can also travel through a solid object, such as a piece of metal, or a gas, such as the air. It cannot travel through a vacuum such as space.

Another type of wave is an electromagnetic wave. This type of wave transfers **electromagnetic radiation**, a type of energy. Examples of electromagnetic radiation include visible light, radio waves, X-rays, and microwaves. Like a mechanical wave, electromagnetic waves transfer energy. However, electromagnetic waves are unique in that they can travel without a medium.

Both types of waves involve a transfer of energy without a transfer of matter. While mechanical waves travel *through* matter, the waves themselves do not move the matter to a new place. The waves are disturbances in matter that transfer energy.

Figure 1 shows several different types of waves at work. Ocean waves cause the buoy to bob in the water. If a seafloor sensor detects a wave called a tsunami (soo NAH mee), it sends a signal to the buoy, which then sends a radio signal to a satellite orbiting Earth. The signal gets relayed to scientists, who can then warn coastal communities. The sunlight that lights this scene is also made of waves.

Reflect Write down some examples of waves that you are familiar with from everyday life. Can you classify them as mechanical or electromagnetic?

World of Waves
Figure 1 A tsunameter is a buoy anchored to the ocean floor. It detects extremely large waves called tsunamis and sends a radio signal to warn people.

Transverse Waves

Waves can be classified by how energy is transmitted. Energy is transmitted through a medium by mechanical waves. Electromagnetic waves are capable of transmitting energy through empty space.

Waves can also be classified by how the particles in a disturbance vibrate. A mechanical wave begins when a source of energy causes a medium to vibrate. The direction of the vibration determines what type of mechanical wave is produced. A **transverse wave** travels perpendicular (at right angles) to the direction of the source's motion. The person in **Figure 2** is using his arms to make up-and-down vibrations in two ropes. Each particle of the rope moves up and down. The direction of the waves he's producing, though, is perpendicular to that up-and-down motion. The energy travels toward the far ends of the ropes.

The curved shape of the rope indicates the main features of a transverse wave. The high point of a wave is its crest, and the low point is the trough. Halfway between the crest and trough is the wave's resting position. The distance between the highest crest and the resting position marks the wave's **amplitude**. In general, the amplitude of a wave is the maximum distance the medium vibrates from the rest position.

Electromagnetic waves, such as sunlight, are also transverse waves. In their case, however, there is no motion of particles, even when light travels through a liquid, such as water, or a solid, such as glass.

Transverse Waves

Figure 2 ✏ Use arrows to indicate the direction the rope is vibrating and the direction energy is flowing. Label a crest and a trough, and indicate the amplitude.

Longitudinal Waves

A wave that travels in the same direction as the vibrations that produce it is called a **longitudinal wave**. Sound is a longitudinal wave. Sound travels from speakers when flat surfaces inside the speakers vibrate in and out, compressing and expanding the air next to them.

Figure 3 shows a longitudinal wave in a spring toy. When the left hand pulls on the toy, the result is a series of stretches and compressions. Gaps between compressions are called rarefactions. Energy moves to the right along the toy.

While the wave travels, the spring particles do not move all the way to the right like the wave does. Each spring particle moves back and forth, like the hand. The small piece of ribbon on the spring moves the same way the particles in the spring move.

Literacy Connection

Integrate Information As you learn about waves, take notes that summarize and categorize the different motions that waves produce.

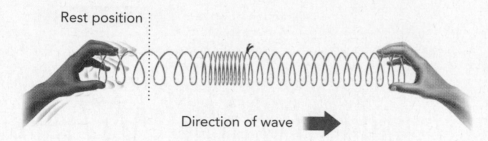

Rest position

Direction of wave ➡️

Longitudinal Wave
Figure 3 🖊 Label a compression and a rarefaction.

Surface Waves

Combinations of transverse and longitudinal waves are called surface waves. For example, an ocean wave travels at the surface of water. When a wave passes through water, the water (and anything on it) vibrates up and down. The water also moves back and forth slightly in the direction that the wave is traveling. The up-and-down and back-and-forth movements combine to make each particle of water move in a circle, as shown in **Figure 4**.

Wave direction

Ball's motion

READING CHECK **Compare and Contrast** What is the main difference between a surface wave and a longitudinal wave?

A longitudinal wave is a wave that travels in the same direction.

Surface Wave
Figure 4 As waves move from left to right, they cause the ball to move in a circle.

Properties of Waves

Figure 5 All waves have amplitude, wavelength, frequency, and speed. After you read about these properties, answer the questions on the image.

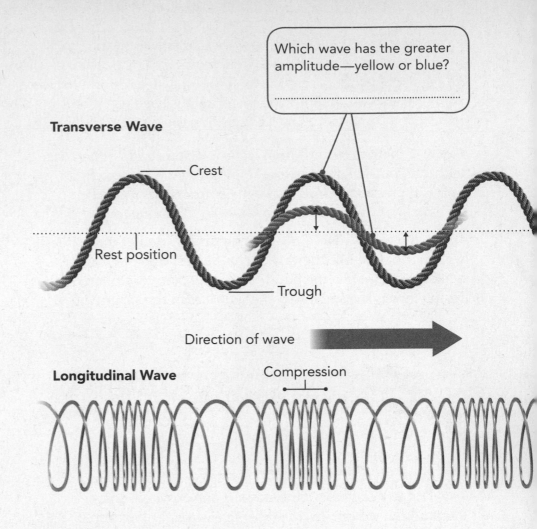

Which wave has the greater amplitude—yellow or blue?

....

Transverse Wave

Crest

Rest position

Trough

Direction of wave

Longitudinal Wave

Compression

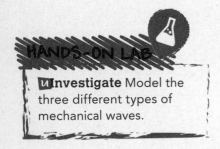

HANDS-ON LAB

uInvestigate Model the three different types of mechanical waves.

INTERACTIVITY

See how a wave travels through a coil.

Properties of Waves

In addition to amplitude, all waves have three other properties: wavelength, frequency, and speed. These properties are all related to one another.

Wavelength Suppose that a wave repeats as it travels. Its **wavelength** is determined by the distance it travels before it starts to repeat. The wavelength of a transverse wave is the distance from crest to crest, as shown in **Figure 5**. For a longitudinal wave, the wavelength is the distance from one compression to the next.

Frequency The number of times a wave repeats in a given amount of time is called its **frequency**. You can also think of frequency as the number of waves that pass a given point in a certain amount of time. For example, if you make waves on a rope so that one wave passes by a point every second, the frequency is 1 wave per second. Frequency is measured in units called hertz (Hz). A wave that occurs every second has a frequency of 1 Hz. If two waves pass by in a second, the frequency is 2 Hz.

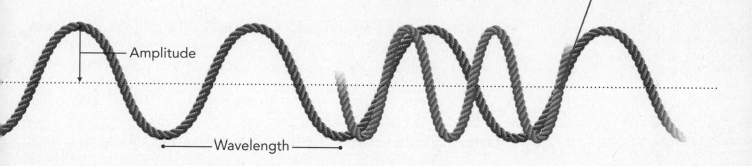

One yellow wave passes by this point each second, so the frequency of the yellow wave is ....

Two green waves pass by this point each second, so the frequency of the green wave is ....

Amplitude

Wavelength

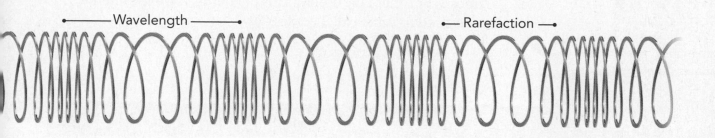

Wavelength

Rarefaction

Speed

The speed of a wave is determined by the distance it travels in a certain amount of time. Different waves have different speeds. For instance, a light wave travels almost a million times faster than a sound wave travels through air! Waves also travel at different speeds through different materials. For example, light travels faster through water than through glass. Sound travels more than three times faster through water than through air.

To calculate a wave's speed, divide the distance it travels by the time it takes to travel that distance. You can also find a wave's speed if you know its wavelength and frequency—just multiply wavelength times frequency.

Wave speed = Wavelength × Frequency

INTERACTIVITY

Generate virtual waves in a wave pool.

✓ READING CHECK **Predict** If you and a friend are standing at opposite ends of a gymnasium and one of you claps, will the other person hear the clap at the same time she sees it happen? Why or why not?

They will here it because the sound will travel across the gym.

See what happens when balls of different masses are dropped in water.

Wave Energy

Waves transmit energy from place to place. The amount of energy they transmit depends on how much energy was input by the original source of the vibration. Faster vibrations transmit more energy. Larger amplitude vibrations also transmit more energy.

In mathematical terms, a wave's energy is directly proportional to frequency. When the frequency of the wave doubles, the energy also doubles. So, if you shake a rope up and down twice as fast, you transmit twice as much energy down the length of the rope.

Mathematically, a wave's energy is also proportional to the square of its amplitude. For instance, if you shake a rope to make waves and then move your hand three times as high with each shake, the wave energy increases by a factor of 3 times 3, or nine! Like other forms of energy, a wave's energy is measured in units called joules (J).

Math Toolbox

Wave Properties

✏ The table shows the properties of waves near the beach on one summer day. Use the relationship between speed, wavelength, and frequency to complete the table. Then answer the questions.

Waves at a Beach				
Time	Amplitude	Wavelength	Frequency	Speed
10 AM	0.4 m	10 m	2 Hz	
2 PM	0.2 m		4 Hz	32 m/s
6 PM	0.3 m	12 m		34 m/s

1. **Use Tables** What would happen to the energy of the 10 AM wave if the frequency increased to 6 Hz?

....

2. **Apply Mathematics** If the amplitude of the 6 PM wave increases to 0.6 m, how many times greater would the energy become?

....

3. **Use Proportional Relationships** Recall that speed = wavelength × frequency. Assuming that the wavelength of a wave stays the same, would the energy of the wave increase or decrease if the speed of the wave increases? Why?

....

....

....

MS-PS4-1

1. **Explain** How can you measure the wave-length of a longitudinal wave?

....

....

....

2. **Calculate** A sound wave's frequency is 4 Hz and its wavelength is 8 meters. What is the wave's speed?

....

3. **Use Models** 🖊 Draw a model of a transverse wave. Use lines and labels to show the amplitude and wavelength of the wave.

4. **Use Proportional Relationships** During high tide, ocean waves often become larger. If the amplitude of a wave increases by a factor of 4, by how much does the energy increase?

....

....

....

5. **Cause and Effect** If a musician increases the wavelength of the sound waves she produces without changing their speed, what must be happening to the frequency? Explain your answer.

....

....

....

....

....

....

....

....

....

Quest CHECK-IN

In this lesson, you learned about the difference between electromagnetic and mechanical waves, including the three different types of mechanical waves that move through and affect the matter around us. You also learned how the properties of waves such as amplitude, frequency, energy, and speed are related.

Evaluate If you were designing a security system that uses light to detect an intruder, why would it be important to know about the different media and materials that would be parts of the system?

....

....

INTERACTIVITY

Light Behavior

Go online to learn more about the behavior of light, including how a mirror affects a laser beam.

MS-PS4-2

SOUND AND LIGHT AT THE
Ballpark

It's baseball season! The lights illuminate the field. As the batter swings, there is a whoosh of the bat through the air, and a satisfying CRACK! as he hits a long ball to the outfield.

Fans are yelling and cheering. "PEANUTS! Get your PEANUTS!" shout the vendors as they move through the packed stands. "Take Me Out to the Ball Game" blares over the speakers, and everyone stands up and sings.

A baseball game is a sporting event. But everything that happens there obeys the laws of physics. How do light and sound waves behave at the ball park? Take a look—and listen!

There are runners on all the bases, and the batter hits the ball. It's a ground ball to the shortstop. He throws it to the third baseman, who has his foot on third base. The umpire at third base watches the runner's foot touch the base while listening for the sound of the ball striking the third baseman's glove.

The next batter comes up to the plate and misses the first pitch. You see the catcher catch the ball before you hear the thwack of the ball hitting his glove.

You see the umpire signal a strike before you hear him call "STRIKE ONE!"

On the next pitch, you hear the crack of the bat hitting the ball after you see the batter hit the ball. It's a home run!

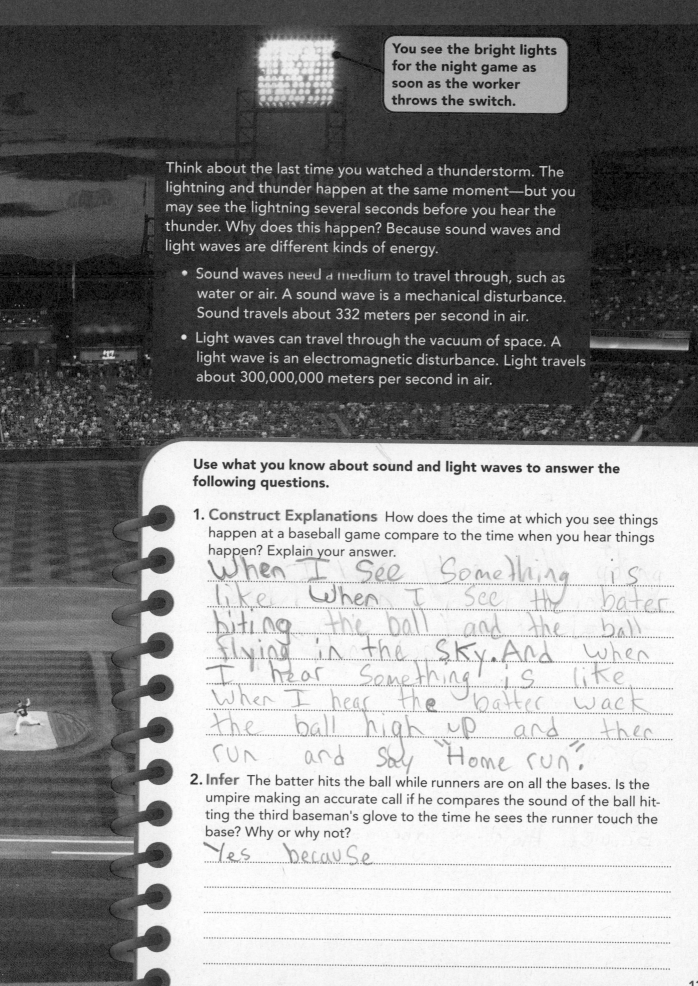

You see the bright lights for the night game as soon as the worker throws the switch.

Think about the last time you watched a thunderstorm. The lightning and thunder happen at the same moment—but you may see the lightning several seconds before you hear the thunder. Why does this happen? Because sound waves and light waves are different kinds of energy.

- Sound waves need a medium to travel through, such as water or air. A sound wave is a mechanical disturbance. Sound travels about 332 meters per second in air.

- Light waves can travel through the vacuum of space. A light wave is an electromagnetic disturbance. Light travels about 300,000,000 meters per second in air.

Use what you know about sound and light waves to answer the following questions.

1. **Construct Explanations** How does the time at which you see things happen at a baseball game compare to the time when you hear things happen? Explain your answer.

   When I see something is like when I see the bater hiting the ball and the ball flying in the sky. And when I hear something is like when I hear the batter wack the ball high up and then run and say "Home run".

2. **Infer** The batter hits the ball while runners are on all the bases. Is the umpire making an accurate call if he compares the sound of the ball hitting the third baseman's glove to the time he sees the runner touch the base? Why or why not?

   Yes because

② Wave Interactions

Guiding Questions

- How do waves interact with different materials?
- How do waves interact with each other?

Connection

Literacy Integrate Information

MS-PS4-2

HANDS-ON LAB

uInvestigate See what type of interference you get when you send waves down a coil.

Vocabulary

reflection
refraction
diffraction
absorption
interference
standing wave
resonance

Academic Vocabulary

transmitted

Connect It!

✏ **Look at the goldfish shown swimming in a glass tank. Place an X on any fish that you think is a reflection.**

Use Evidence How many real fish do you think there are?

2 fish.

Construct Explanations Why is it difficult to count the number of fish in the tank?

Because their is glass around them / mirror.

Reflection, Refraction, and Absorption

If you've ever been to the beach, you've seen how different kinds of waves move. Some ocean waves crash into rocks or piers, while others reach the shore smoothly. Rays of sunlight hit the surface of the water, and some bounce off while others pass through. In general, when waves encounter different media, they are either reflected, transmitted, or absorbed.

Reflection Some waves are completely blocked by an obstruction, but their energy is not absorbed or converted to another form of energy. These types of waves bounce off, or reflect from, those obstructions. In a <mark>reflection</mark>, the wave bounces off and heads in a different direction. The law of reflection states that the angle of incidence equals the angle of reflection. This means that the angle at which the wave strikes the material will match the angle at which the reflected wave bounces off that material, as shown in **Figure 2**. Light reflecting from a mirror is the most familiar example of reflection. The echo of a voice from the walls of a canyon is another example.

Reflection

Figure 2 A flashlight beam reflects off of a mirror at the same angle it strikes.

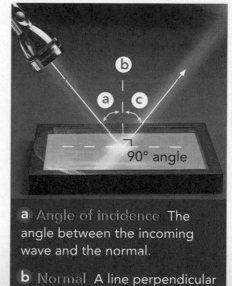

90° angle

a Angle of incidence The angle between the incoming wave and the normal.

b Normal A line perpendicular to the surface at the point where reflection occurs.

c Angle of reflection The angle between the reflected wave and the normal.

Fish Reflection and Refraction

Figure 1 Light waves reflecting off the walls of a tank can create multiple images of the same fish.

Develop Models ✎ Have you ever seen a movie scene in which a character appears to be looking at a mirror, yet the camera is not visible in the mirror? Think about how the director sets up this scene. Draw a set up that shows the position of the actor, the camera, and the mirror, and demonstrate why the camera's image is not visible to the camera.

Refraction

Figure 3 Light rays bend as they enter water because one side of the wave fronts slows down in water while the other side continues at the same speed in air.

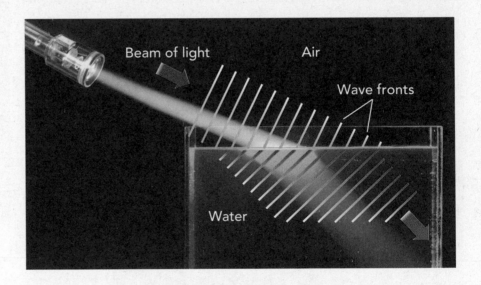

What is another way for saying that a wave is "transmitted" through a medium?

....

....

....

Refraction

Imagine riding a bike down a smooth asphalt road. When you turn off the road onto a dirt path, the transition can be jarring. You might have to grip the handlebars hard to keep the bike going straight as each wheel is on a different surface.

When light waves are **transmitted** from one medium into another, they also bend in different directions. This bending is due to **refraction**, or the bending of waves due to a change in speed.

When a wave enters a new medium at an angle other than perpendicular, it changes direction. For instance, when light is directed at water at an angle, as in **Figure 3**, the light slows down and bends downward. The wave bends toward the normal, the imaginary line that runs perpendicular from the boundary between the two media.

Diffraction Did you ever wonder how you can hear someone speaking even if they are around the corner of a building or doorway? This is an example of diffraction. Waves don't only travel in straight lines. They are also bend around objects.

You can observe diffraction with water waves as well as sound waves. Water waves can diffract around a rock or an island in the ocean. Because tsunami waves can diffract all the way around an island, people on the shores of the entire island are at risk.

Absorption When you think of something being absorbed, you might think of how a paper towel soaks up water. Waves can be absorbed by certain materials, too. In absorption, the energy of a wave is transferred to the material it encounters. When ocean waves reach a shoreline, most of their energy is absorbed by the shore.

When light waves encounter the surface of a different medium or material, the light waves may be reflected, refracted, or absorbed. What happens to the waves depends on the type of material they hit. Light is mostly absorbed by dark materials, such as the surface of a parking lot, and mostly reflected by light materials, such as snow.

Literacy Connection

Integrate Information
As you read, classify the phenomena you learn about as either interactions between waves and media or interactions among waves.

Reflect What are some ways in which you use reflection in your everyday life? Are there things you have to keep in mind when you use reflective devices, such as mirrors?

▶ VIDEO
Discover how reflection and absorption create echoes.

Question It!

Classify ✏ Identify each picture as being an example of reflection, refraction, or absorption.

Dixxraction   reflection   Absorption   reflection

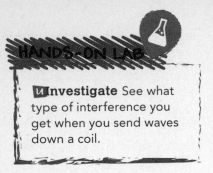

Wave Interference

Have you ever seen two ocean waves collide from opposite directions so they momentarily form a bigger, hill-like shape before continuing in their original directions? This is an example of wave **interference**. There are two types.

Constructive Interference

The example of two waves of similar sizes colliding and forming a wave with an amplitude greater than either of the original waves is called constructive interference. You can think of it as waves "helping each other," or adding their energies together. As shown in **Figure 4**, when the crests of two waves overlap, they make a higher crest. If two troughs overlap, they make a deeper trough. In both cases, the amplitude of the combined crests or troughs increases.

Types of Interference

Figure 4 🖊 Write captions to describe three parts of destructive interference. Complete the key to explain what the different arrows mean in the images.

Constructive Interference

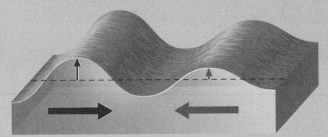

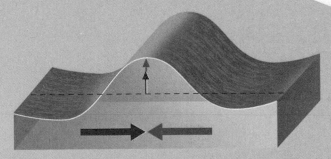

❶ Two waves approach each other. The wave on the left has a greater amplitude.

❷ The new crest's amplitude is the sum of the amplitudes of the original crests.

Destructive Interference

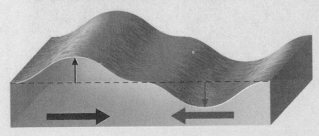

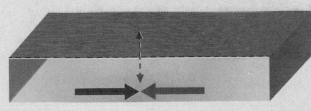

❶ ....

....

❷ ....

....

Destructive Interference

When two waves combine to form a wave with a smaller amplitude than either original wave had, this is called destructive interference. Destructive interference occurs when the crest of one wave overlaps the trough of another wave. If the crest has a larger amplitude than the trough of the other wave, the crest "wins," and part of it remains. If the original trough has a larger amplitude than the crest of the other wave, the result is a trough. If a crest and trough have equal amplitudes, they cancel each other out, as shown in **Figure 4**. Destructive interference is used in noise-canceling headphones to block out distracting noises in a listener's surroundings.

READING CHECK **Infer** Which type of wave interference could cause sound to become louder? Explain your answer.

....

....

....

INTERACTIVITY

Observe wave interference in a rope and in surface waves.

Interfering Waves

Figure 5 Ripples created by rain water on a pond interfere with one another in a pattern that exhibits both constructive and destructive interference.

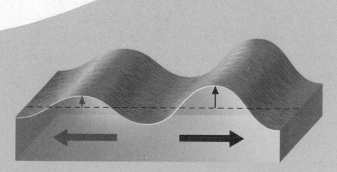

❸ The waves continue as if they had not met.

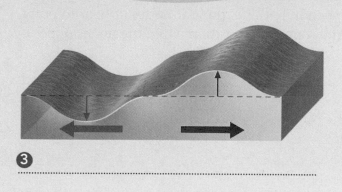

❸

....

....

Key
→
←
↑
↓

Standing Waves

Figure 6 🖊 As the hand shown at left increases the frequency, the number of wavelengths present in the standing wave will increase. In a standing wave, it looks like there's a mirror image of both the crest and trough. Label the rest of the nodes and antinodes.

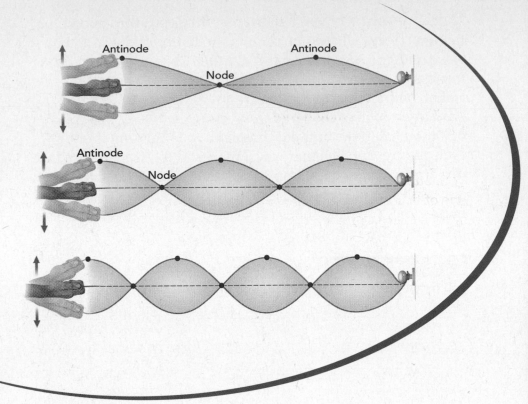

INTERACTIVITY

Describe how waves behave when they interact with a barrier or boundary.

Standing Waves

Look at the rope setup in **Figure 6.** The rope is tied to a doorknob, and someone shakes the free end. This motion can generate standing waves. A **standing wave** is a wave that appears to stand in one place. Standing waves are produced by two waves interfering with each other as they travel in opposite directions. Standing waves on the rope appear when an incoming wave and wave reflected from the doorknob have just the right frequency to interfere as shown.

In a standing wave, destructive interference between the two colliding waves produces points with zero amplitude, called nodes. The nodes are always evenly spaced along the wave. Points of maximum amplitude on a standing wave are called antinodes. Antinodes always occur halfway between two nodes. The frequency and wavelength of the interfering waves determine how many nodes and antinodes the standing wave will have. When seen in real life, the antinodes appear to pulse in and out from the rope's rest position while the nodes appear motionless.

Standing waves can sometimes appear on lakes when the wind and pressure around them are just right. The water appears to have a node in the center of the lake, and the water wave rolls around that node.

Resonance Think about the last time you swung on a swing at a playground. You may have noticed that it is difficult to get yourself going. Once you are in motion, you can pull on the chains of the swing and pump your legs at the right time to keep yourself swinging. The swing has a natural frequency, and your actions match that frequency to create greater amplitudes in your motion.

Most objects have at least one natural frequency of vibration. Standing waves occur in an object when it vibrates at one of these natural frequencies. If a nearby object vibrates at the same frequency, it can cause resonance. **Resonance** is an increase in the amplitude of a vibration that occurs when external vibrations match an object's natural frequency.

When engineers build a bridge, they have to make sure that bridge supports are not placed at potential nodes for a standing wave. Otherwise, wind could cause the bridge to swing wildly like the rope in **Figure 6** and collapse.

Understanding the resonance of different materials is also useful for people who build guitars, violins, or other wood-based stringed instruments. If the wood in a guitar, such as the one in **Figure 7**, resonates too much with a certain note, it may sound too loud when that particular note is struck. Likewise, if the wood does not resonate with any particular note, the instrument may lack volume or "presence" and sound dull.

☑ **READING CHECK** **Summarize** In general, why is it risky to build something whose natural frequency can be matched by external vibrations?

....

....

....

📓 **Make Meaning** Make a two-column chart in your notebook. Use it to record descriptions of constructive interference, destructive interference, standing waves, and resonance.

Musical Resonance
Figure 7 The types of wood and construction techniques used to make a guitar affect aspects of its sound, including its resonance.

1. Relate Cause and Effect Explain what happens to light when it is refracted at the surface of water.

....

....

....

....

....

2. Interpret Diagrams The diagrams below show two waves interfering to form a dark blue result. Which of the diagrams depicts constructive interference? Explain your choice using the term *amplitude*.

A. ➡   B. ➡   ⬅

....

....

....

....

3. Explain What does it mean for waves to be absorbed by a certain medium? Make sure to include energy in your explanation.

....

....

....

....

4. Construct Explanations Why does the transition of light waves from water to air make it seem as if fish and other things in a pond are shallower than they actually are?

....

....

....

....

....

....

....

....

....

....

....

....

Quest CHECK-IN

In this lesson, you learned how waves interact with their surroundings and with each other. Waves can reflect, refract, and be absorbed depending on the media they travel through and the materials they strike. They can also interfere with each other in ways that are destructive or constructive, resulting in phenomena such as standings waves and resonance.

Apply Concepts Think about the ways that light can change direction. What are two ways that you could change the path of light? What materials would you need to do it?

....

....

....

Say "CHEESE!"

▶ VIDEO

Find out how cameras work.

For hundreds of years, people who traveled took sketch pads and pencils to record their memories. This all changed in the nineteenth century with the invention of photography.

▶ The Challenge To continue to improve the ways in which people can record images.

Phenomenon Early cameras were large and clumsy objects that printed images on glass. In the twentieth century, engineers experimented with smaller and lighter cameras that used film. Today we have digital cameras. But they all use the same process to create images.

Today, cameras all have three main parts for capturing light:

- The **lens** is the camera's eye. It detects the light reflected off of what you want to photograph.

- The **aperture** lets light in through the lens. The wider the aperture, the more light is let in.

- The **shutter** is like a curtain that opens when you take the photo.

In a film camera, the light changes the film both physically and chemically to create an image. In a *digital* camera, the light reaches photosensors, which convert the image to a string of numbers.

Cameras have changed a lot over the years!

DESIGN CHALLENGE Can you build your own simple camera using just a box? Go to the Engineering Design Notebook to find out!

3 Sound Waves

Guiding Questions

- How are sound waves reflected, transmitted, or absorbed by materials?
- What factors affect the speed of sound waves?

Connections

Literacy Integrate With Visuals

Math Reason Quantitatively

MS-PS4-2

HANDS-ON LAB

uInvestigate Use models to examine how sound waves travel through different media.

Vocabulary

loudness
intensity
decibel
pitch
Doppler effect

Academic Vocabulary

differentiate

Connect It

✏️ **When someone strikes a cymbal, the cymbal vibrates to produce sound. Draw compressions and rarefactions of the air particles as the sound waves travel away from the cymbal.**

Ask Questions Is sound a mechanical wave or an electromagnetic wave? Explain your answer.

....

Predict What do you think happens to a sound wave when the volume of sound increases?

....

The Behavior of Sound

All sound waves begin with a vibration. Look at the woman in **Figure 1.** When she hits a drum or a cymbal with her drumstick, the drum or cymbal vibrates rapidly, disturbing the air particles around the drum set. When the drum or cymbal moves away from its rest position, it creates a compression by pushing air particles together. When it moves back toward its rest position, it creates a rarefaction by causing air particles to spread out.

Recall that sound waves are mechanical waves that require a medium through which to travel. In the case of the drummer and the drum set, the compressions and rarefactions that are created travel through the air. Sound waves, however, travel more easily through liquids and solids. When you set a glass down on a table, for example, the sound waves that are generated travel first through the glass and the table and then are released into the air.

Sound waves are also longitudinal—they travel in the same direction as the vibrations that produce them. Like other types of mechanical waves, sound waves can be reflected, transmitted, absorbed, and diffracted.

HANDS-ON LAB

Discover how the amplitude of a guitar string affects its loudness.

Making Waves
Figure 1 The vibrations caused by hitting drums and cymbals generate sound waves.

INTERACTIVITY

Observe and analyze sound waves in a variety of everyday situations.

Reflection and Transmission

Like other mechanical waves, sound waves that pass through a surface are called transmitted waves, and sound waves that bounce off a surface are called reflected waves. When a sound wave travels through the air and comes into contact with a solid surface, such as a wall, a portion of the wave passes through the surface. Most of the wave, however, is reflected away from the surface.

Absorption

Have you ever been to a concert in a large indoor theater? If so, you may have noticed panels on the walls. Most large theaters have acoustic panels to help with sound absorption. Sound absorption describes the process of sound waves striking a surface and quickly losing energy. The energy is converted to thermal energy in the surface. Acoustic panels in theaters are porous, meaning they are full of small holes, and they absorb a portion of the sound waves. In the case of a theater, absorption of sound waves improves the listening experience for people at the concert. More sound energy is absorbed than reflected, so the audience does not experience as much interference from reflected sound waves. See **Figure 2** for another example of absorption. Any material with a porous surface can act as a sound absorber.

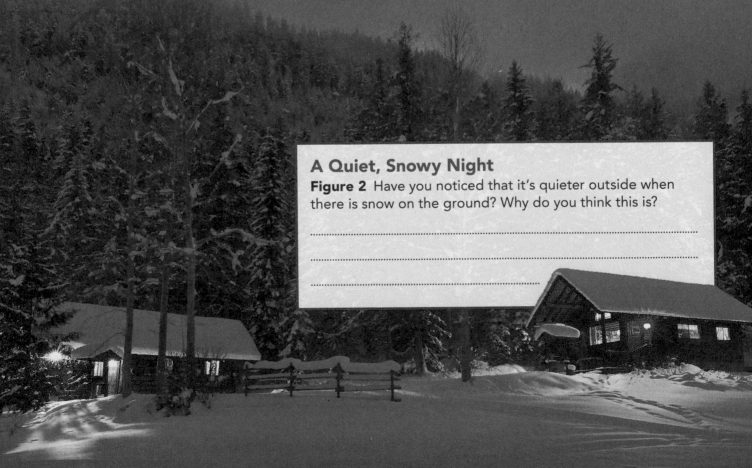

A Quiet, Snowy Night

Figure 2 Have you noticed that it's quieter outside when there is snow on the ground? Why do you think this is?

....

....

....

Model It

If you've ever yelled loudly into an open space, such as a canyon or a courtyard, then you may have heard an echo. An echo occurs when sound waves are reflected off a hard surface, such as the wall of a rocky mountain. The sound you hear is delayed because it takes time for the sound waves to reflect off the surface and reach your ears.

Develop Models 🖉 Draw a picture of sound waves when an echo is created. In addition to reflected waves, your model should also indicate waves that are transmitted or absorbed.

Diffraction
It is usually easy to hear someone talking if they are in the same room as you, but you can also hear people in other rooms nearby. Why is this? You can hear them because sound waves can bend around the edges of an opening, such as a doorway. This is called sound diffraction. Sound waves, like water waves, spread out after passing through an opening.

How much sound waves are transmitted, reflected, absorbed, or diffracted depends greatly upon the medium through which they travel. If sound waves travel through air and hit a solid surface, such as a concrete wall, much of the energy in the waves is reflected back toward the source. If the surfaces they hit are softer or more porous, then more sound waves will be absorbed. Sound waves will be diffracted around corners and through passageways between hard surfaces.

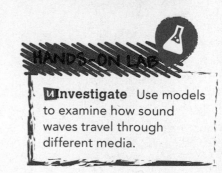

HANDS-ON LAB

u**Investigate** Use models to examine how sound waves travel through different media.

✓ **READING CHECK** **Summarize** What are four things that can happen to sound waves when they reach a barrier?

....

....

VIDEO

Explore what thunder is and how to determine your distance from an approaching storm.

Speed of Sound

Figure 3 Rate the speed of sound through the medium in each container, with "1" being the fastest and "3" being the slowest.

Factors Affecting the Speed of Sound

As you have read, sound waves are mechanical waves that require a medium through which to travel. The characteristics of the medium have an effect on the speed of the sound waves traveling through them. The main factors that affect the speed of sound are compressibility, stiffness, density, and temperature.

Stiffness In general, sound waves travel faster in materials that are harder to compress. This is because of how efficiently the movement of one particle will push on another. Think of the coins, water, and air in **Figure 3**. Solids are less compressible than liquids, which are less compressible than gases. Therefore, sound waves travel fastest in solids and slowest in gases.

For solids, stiffness is also important. Sound travels faster in stiffer solids, such as metals, than in less rigid solids, such as pudding.

Density The density of the medium also affects the speed of sound waves. Density refers to how much matter or mass there is in a given amount of space. The denser the material, the more mass it has in a given volume, so the greater its inertia. Objects with greater inertia accelerate less from an energy disturbance than objects with less inertia, or less massive objects. Therefore, in materials of the same stiffness, sound travels more slowly in the denser material.

Temperature The temperature of a medium also affects the speed at which sound waves travel through it, though in more complicated ways. For solids, an increase in temperature reduces the stiffness, so the sound speed decreases. For fluids, such as air, the increase in temperature reduces the density, so the sound speed generally increases.

☑ READING CHECK **Hypothesize** Would sound waves travel slower through air at the North Pole or at the equator? Explain.

....

....

....

....

....

Loudness and Pitch

How might you describe a sound? You might call it loud or soft, high or low. When you turn up the volume of your speakers, you increase the loudness of a sound. When you sing higher and higher notes, you increase the pitch of your voice. Loudness and pitch depend on different properties of sound waves.

Factors Affecting Loudness You use the term loudness to describe your awareness of the energy of a sound. How loud a sound is depends on the energy and intensity of the sound waves. If someone knocks lightly on your front door, then you might hear a quiet sound. If they pound on your door, then you hear a much louder sound. Why? The pounding transfers much more energy through the door than a light knock does. That's because a hard knock on a door produces a much greater amplitude in the sound waves than a softer knock does. Increased energy results in greater intensity of the waves. Intensity is the amount of energy a sound wave carries per second through a unit area. The closer the sound wave is to its source, the more energy it has in a given area. As the sound wave moves away from the source, the wave spreads out and the intensity decreases.

INTERACTIVITY

Explore how the frequency and intensity of a sound wave affect the sound you hear through headphones.

Intensity of Sound

Figure 4 Sound waves spread out as they travel away from the source producing the sound. For each of the locations in the image, rank the intensity of the sound waves coming from the band on a scale of 1 to 3, with 1 being the greatest intensity.

Academic Vocabulary

What is the root word in *differentiate*? How does this help you figure out the word's meaning?

....

....

....

....

....

....

Measuring Loudness

So, how do our ears **differentiate** between a light knock and a hard knock on a door? Loudness can be measured by a unit called a **decibel** (dB). The greater the decibels of the sound, the louder that sound seems to a listener. The loudness of a sound you can barely hear, such as a pin dropping to the floor, is about 0 dB. When someone lightly taps on your door, the loudness is about 30 dB. But if someone pounds on your door, that loudness might increase to 80 dB! Sounds louder than 100 dB, such as the sound of a chainsaw, can cause damage to people's ears, especially if they are exposed to the sounds for long periods of time. Music technicians use equalizers to change the loudness levels of different frequencies of sound, as in **Figure 5**.

Using an Equalizer

Figure 5 You can use an equalizer to adjust the loudness of sound waves at different frequencies. Raising the decibel level of low frequencies increases the bass tones of music. How might you increase the high-pitched tones of music?

....

....

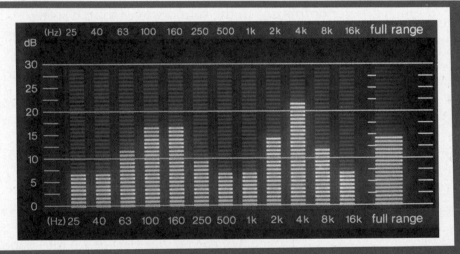

Math Toolbox

Decibel Levels

Every 10-decibel increase represents a tenfold increase in intensity and power. For example, when loudness increases from 20 to 30 decibels, a sound's power is multiplied by 10. If loudness increases by 10 again, power increases by another factor of 10. Therefore, when loudness increases from 20 to 40 decibels, power increases by a factor of 100!

1. **Reason Quantitatively** If a sound's power level increases from 20 decibels to 50 decibels, by what factor does its power increase?

....

....

2. **Cause and Effect** If you want to lower the loudness of the bass tones in your music by 20 decibels, by how much does the intensity need to decrease?

....

Thickness Affects Pitch

Figure 6 On a standard 6-string guitar, the strings range in thickness.

✏ On the photo, draw an X on the guitar string that has the lowest pitch.

Factors Affecting Pitch Have you ever heard someone describe a note on a piano as "high-pitched" or "low-pitched"? The pitch of a sound refers to how high or low the sound seems. Pitch depends upon the frequency of the sound waves. Sound waves with a high frequency have a high pitch, and waves with a low frequency have a low pitch.

The frequency of a sound wave depends upon how fast the source of the sound is vibrating. For example, when people speak or sing, the air from their lungs moves past their vocal cords and makes the cords vibrate, producing sound waves. When vocal cords vibrate more quickly, they produce higher-frequency sound waves with higher pitches. When vocal cords vibrate more slowly, they produce lower-frequency sound waves with lower pitches.

This phenomenon happens with all things that vibrate and produce sound waves. Guitars produce sound when someone strums or plucks their strings. If you've ever studied a guitar, then you may have noticed that its strings vary in thickness. The thicker strings of a guitar vibrate more slowly than the thinner strings do, and so the thicker strings have a lower frequency, and therefore a lower pitch, than the thinner strings (**Figure 6**).

INTERACTIVITY

Explain how sounds from moving objects can change in pitch.

Literacy Connection

Integrate With Visuals
Do you think the motorcyclist would hear a change in pitch of the motorcycle's sound as he passes by you? Why or why not?

....

....

....

....

....

The Doppler Effect

Have you ever had a loud motorcycle drive by you and heard the pitch of the engine noise change? Change in pitch occurs because the movement of the source of the sound causes a sound wave to either compress or stretch. As the motorcycle approaches, the peaks of the emitted sound waves are scrunched together. When the peaks are closer together, the sound waves have a higher frequency. As the motorcycle moves away, the peaks of the emitted sound waves are spread out. The sound waves then have a lower frequency.

A change in frequency is perceived by a listener as a change in pitch. This change in frequency (and therefore, in pitch) of the sound wave in relation to an observer is called the **Doppler effect.** **Figure 7** shows the Doppler effect when a firetruck rushes by a person on the sidewalk.

✓ READING CHECK **Summarize** What property of a sound wave determines the pitch of a sound?

....

....

The Doppler Effect

Figure 7 As a firetruck speeds by, an observer detects changes in the pitch of the truck's siren. The firetruck approaches the observer in the first image. It then passes her and continues on.
✏ Draw the sound waves as the truck moves away.

☑ LESSON 3 Check

1. **Identify** What is the cause of any sound wave?

....

....

2. **Construct Explanations** Explain why sound waves are mechanical waves rather than electromagnetic waves.

....

....

....

3. **Apply Scientific Reasoning** Why does sound travel more quickly through a solid than through a liquid or a gas?

....

....

....

....

....

....

4. **Form a Hypothesis** Dogs can hear higher-pitched whistles that humans do. How do you think the sound frequencies that dogs can hear compare to the frequencies that humans can hear?

....

....

....

....

5. **Cause and Effect** What effect might spending years working on a construction site have on a person's hearing? Why?

....

....

....

....

....

....

6. **Apply Concepts** Ultrasound, also known as sonography, is a technology that uses high-frequency sound waves to produce images. It is used in medical applications to help doctors see inside patients' bodies. How do you think the sound waves can be used to image bones, muscles, and other internal structures?

....

....

....

....

....

....

7. **Develop Models** ✏ Imagine a person is sitting on a beach, and a speedboat passes by on the water. Draw a model of this situation, and indicate how the Doppler effect would influence how the sound waves coming from the boat would be perceived by the person on shore.

....

....

....

....

....

LESSON
4 Electromagnetic Waves

Guiding Questions

- What makes up an electromagnetic wave?
- How can you model electromagnetic wave behavior?
- What kinds of waves make up the electromagnetic spectrum?

Connections

Literacy Translate Information

Math Draw Comparative Inferences

MS-PS4-2

HANDS-ON LAB

uInvestigate Develop a model of a wave.

Vocabulary

electromagnetic wave
electromagnetic spectrum
radio waves
microwaves
visible light
ultraviolet rays
infrared rays
X-rays
gamma rays

Academic Vocabulary

transverse

✏️ Look at the image of this ship. Imagine that an airplane some 25 kilometers in front of the ship is sending out radar waves to detect vessels. Recall the law of reflection from Lesson 2. Draw arrows to represent the radar waves and to show how they would reflect off this unusually angular ship.

Infer Do you think the reflected waves would ever return to the airplane that transmitted them? Explain.

....

....

....

Characteristics of Electromagnetic Waves

As you read this book, you are surrounded by waves. There are radio waves, microwaves, infrared rays, visible light, ultraviolet rays, and tiny amounts of X-rays and gamma rays. These waves are all electromagnetic waves. An **electromagnetic wave** is made up of vibrating electric and magnetic fields that can move through space at the speed of light. The energy that electromagnetic waves transfer through matter or space is called electromagnetic radiation.

Electromagnetic waves do not require a medium such as air, so they can transfer energy through a vacuum. This property makes them different from mechanical waves, which do require a medium. Mechanical waves are caused by a disturbance or vibration in the medium, while electromagnetic waves are caused by a source of electric and magnetic fields. Those fields are produced by the movement of charged particles.

Radar is a technology that uses microwaves, a type of electromagnetic wave, to detect objects in the atmosphere. The vessel in **Figure 1** is the U.S. Navy's attempt at using stealth technology to deflect radar. Its angular surface causes the microwaves to deflect away from the radar source.

Reflect Think about the devices you use every day. What are some examples of technology that use electromagnetic waves?

Stealth Ship
Figure 1 *The U.S.S. Zumwalt* is the first in a class of "stealth" destroyers. Much of its hull and other structures have surfaces that are angled upward. This means radar waves will be deflected away from the source of the radar.

The term *transverse* means "situated across." It is always applied to something that has a specific orientation or direction. Is there a part of the term *transverse* that signals this meaning?

....

....

....

....

Models of Electromagnetic Wave Behavior

Light is mysterious in that it can behave as either a wave or a particle depending on the situation. A wave model can explain most of the behaviors, but a particle model best explains others. Light is an electromagnetic wave, which is a transverse wave. Light has many properties of transverse waves, but it can sometimes act as though it is a stream of particles.

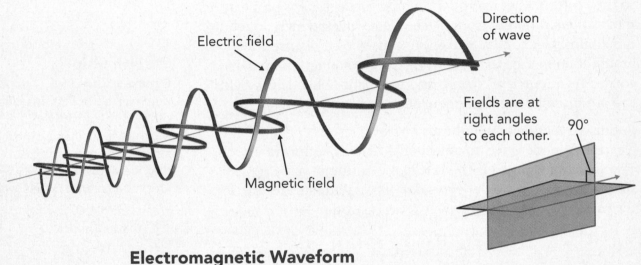

Electric field

Direction of wave

Magnetic field

Fields are at right angles to each other.

90°

Electromagnetic Waveform

Figure 2 An electromagnetic wave consists of vibrating electric and magnetic fields.

INTERACTIVITY

Find out more about the differences between light waves and sound waves.

Wave Model of Light
One way to visualize light is using a wave model. The wave originates due to a disturbance of a charged particle. The disturbance results in vibrating electric and magnetic fields, which are oriented perpendicular to each other as shown in **Figure 2.** The two vibrating fields reinforce each other, causing energy to travel as light through space or through a medium. A ray of light consists of many of these traveling disturbances, vibrating in all directions.

A polarizing filter acts as though it has tiny slits aligned in only one direction. The slits can be horizontal or vertical. When light enters the filter, only waves whose vibrating electric fields are oriented in the same direction as the slits can pass through it. The light that passes through is called polarized light. Polarized sunglasses block out some waves of light so that your eyes are not exposed to as much radiation.

Polarizing Glasses

🖊 These sunglasses allow light through only if the light waves are oriented vertically. Draw the light wave that passes through each lens.

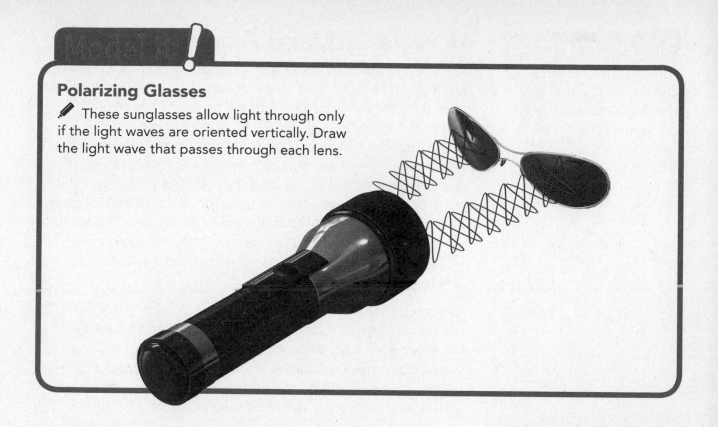

Particle Model of Light

The wave model of light does not explain all of its properties. For example, when a beam of high-frequency light shines on some metals, it knocks some tiny particles called electrons out of the metal. This is called the photoelectric effect. However, lower-frequency light such as red light doesn't have enough energy to knock the electrons out.

The photoelectric effect can be explained by thinking of light as a stream of tiny packets, of energy instead of as a wave. Each packet of light energy is called a photon. For the effect to occur, each photon must contain enough energy to knock an electron free from the metal.

One property of light that the wave model explains but the particle model does not is diffraction. When light passes through a narrow enough slit, instead of forming one image of the slit on a screen, it spreads out and produces a striped pattern of light and dark areas. This is similar to a water wave passing through a narrow channel and then spreading out on the other side.

▶ **VIDEO**

Watch this video to compare the wave and particle models of light.

👆 **INTERACTIVITY**

Explore the particle model of light yourself.

☑ **READING CHECK** **Summarize** Light is described as what two things in the two models you just read about?

....

....

Literacy Connection

Translate Information
How is visible light similar to and different from radio waves?

....

....

....

....

....

....

Wavelength and Frequency

If you use a wave model for electromagnetic waves, the waves have all of the properties that mechanical waves do. Namely, each wave has a certain amplitude, frequency, wavelength, wave speed, and energy. Electromagnetic waves are divided into categories based on their wavelengths (or frequencies). Visible light, radio waves, and X-rays are three examples of electromagnetic waves. But each has properties that make it more useful for some purposes than for others. If you tried to microwave your food with radio waves, or make a phone call with X-rays, you wouldn't get very far! All electromagnetic waves travel at the same speed in a vacuum, but they have different wavelengths and different frequencies.

As you can see in **Figure 3**, wavelength and frequency are related. In order for a wave to have a high frequency, its wavelength must be short. Waves with the shortest wavelengths have the highest frequencies. Frequency is also related to energy. Higher frequency waves have more energy, while lower frequency waves have less energy.

Visible light is the only range of wavelengths your eyes can see. A radio detects radio waves, which have much longer wavelengths than visible light. X-rays, on the other hand, have much shorter wavelengths than visible light.

☑ READING CHECK Draw Conclusions Of X-rays, radio waves, and visible light, which wave type has the most energy? Explain.

....

....

Wavelengths and Frequencies

Figure 3 ✎ Use the information from the text to label the three wavelength ranges shown in the diagram as either X-rays, radio waves, or visible light.

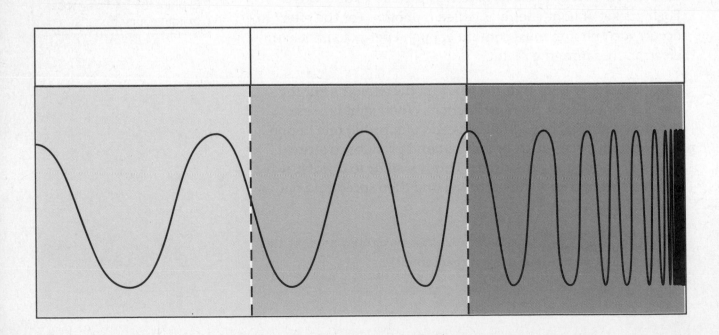

The Electromagnetic Spectrum

There are many different types of electromagnetic waves. The complete range of electromagnetic waves placed in order of increasing frequency is called the electromagnetic spectrum. The electromagnetic spectrum is made up of radio waves, microwaves, infrared rays, visible light, ultraviolet rays, X-rays, and gamma rays. The full spectrum is shown in the Math Toolbox.

Radio Waves
Electromagnetic waves with the longest wavelengths and the lowest frequencies are radio waves. Radio waves are used in mobile phones. Towers, such as the one in **Figure 4**, receive and transmit radio waves along a network that connects mobile phones to each other, to the Internet, and to other networks.

Mobile Phones
Figure 4 Mobile phones depend on a network of towers to transmit, receive, and relay radio signals.

Math Toolbox

Frequencies and Wavelengths of Light

Electromagnetic Spectrum

Visible spectrum

Radio waves | Microwaves | Infrared | Ultraviolet | X-rays | Gamma-rays

LONGER WAVELENGTH   Wavelength (m) decreases ➡   SHORTER WAVELENGTH

10^3 10^2 10^1 1 10^{-1} 10^{-2} 10^{-3} 10^{-4} 10^{-5} 10^{-6} 10^{-7} 10^{-8} 10^{-9} 10^{-10} 10^{-11} 10^{-12} 10^{-13} 10^{-14} 10^{-15}

10^6 10^7 10^8 10^9 10^{10} 10^{11} 10^{12} 10^{13} 10^{14} 10^{15} 10^{16} 10^{17} 10^{18} 10^{19} 10^{20} 10^{21} 10^{22} 10^{23}

Lower Frequency   Frequency (Hz) increases ➡   Higher Frequency

Use the electromagnetic spectrum to answer the following questions.

1. Draw Comparative Inferences
Which has a higher frequency: microwaves or blue light? How do you know?

....

....

....

2. Interpret Visuals If a certain electromagnetic wave has a wavelength of 100 m, what type of electromagnetic wave is it? How do you know?

....

....

....

Microwaves

Microwaves have shorter wavelengths and higher frequencies than radio waves. When you think about microwaves, you probably think of microwave ovens. But microwaves have many other uses, including radar. Radar is a system that uses reflected microwaves to detect objects and measure their distance and speed. Radar guns, such as the one in **Figure 5**, are used to measure the speed of a baseball pitch. Police also use them to detect cars that are traveling over the speed limit.

Infrared Rays

If you turn on an electric stove's burner, you can feel it warm up before the heating element starts to glow. The invisible heat you feel is infrared radiation, or infrared rays. **Infrared rays** are electromagnetic waves with wavelengths shorter than those of microwaves. An infrared camera uses infrared rays instead of visible light to take pictures called thermograms, such as the one in **Figure 6**.

Visible Light

Electromagnetic waves that you can see are called **visible light**. Visible light waves have shorter wavelengths and higher frequencies than infrared rays.

Recall that light waves bend, or refract, when they enter a new medium, such as water or glass. Light from the sun contains electromagnetic waves of many frequencies, both visible and invisible. Sunlight passing through a prism splits into its different frequencies, forming a rainbow pattern. After rainy conditions, rainbows such as the one in **Figure 7** can also form in the sky.

Lighting Up the Radar Gun

Figure 5 Radar guns are used in law enforcement to stop speeding drivers, but they are also used to measure the speeds of pitches in a game of baseball. Some pitchers' fastballs have been clocked at 105 miles per hour!

HANDS-ON LAB

ʊInvestigate Develop a model of a wave.

Thermogram

Figure 6 Label the blank spaces rectangles on the thermogram with temperatures in degrees Celsius.

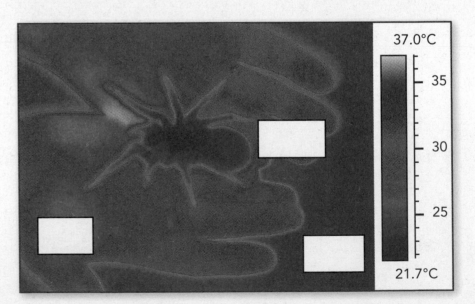

Ultraviolet Rays Electromagnetic waves with wavelengths just shorter than those of visible light are called ultraviolet rays, or UV rays for short. UV rays have higher frequencies than visible light, and carry more energy. Sunscreen helps protect your skin from some of the sun's harmful UV rays.

X-rays Electromagnetic waves with wavelengths shorter than those of ultraviolet rays are X-rays. Because of their high frequencies, X-rays carry more energy than ultraviolet rays and can penetrate most matter. However, dense matter, such as bone, absorbs X-rays. Therefore, X-rays are used to make images of bones and teeth in humans and animals.

Gamma Rays Electromagnetic waves with the shortest wavelengths and highest frequencies are gamma rays. They have the greatest amount of energy of all the electromagnetic waves. Gamma rays are dangerous, but they do have beneficial uses. Radiosurgery shown in **Figure 8,** is a tool that uses several hundred precisely focused gamma rays to target tumors, especially in the brain. The blast of radiation at the point where the beams cross destroys the targeted tumor cells.

Rainbow
Figure 7 Label the rainbow to show which colors have the highest frequency and which have the lowest frequency.

INTERACTIVITY

Observe how electromagnetic and mechanical waves differ.

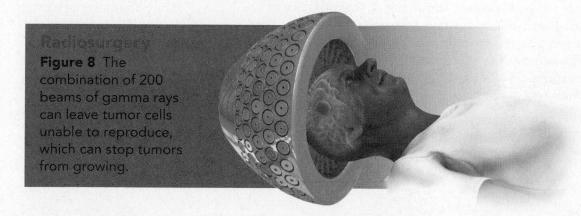
Radiosurgery
Figure 8 The combination of 200 beams of gamma rays can leave tumor cells unable to reproduce, which can stop tumors from growing.

READING CHECK **Draw Conclusions** Can radio waves be used to form images of your bones like x-rays are? Why or why not?

....

....

MS-PS4-2

1. Organize Information In order from lowest to highest frequency, list the different waves along the electromagnetic spectrum.

....
....
....
....
....
....

2. Summarize Describe the electromagnetic spectrum in a few sentences.

....
....
....
....
....
....

3. Explain Compare the particle model of light to the wave model of light.

....
....
....
....
....

4. Connect to Society How would you describe the connection between the amount of energy a type of electromagnetic wave has and how that wave is used in technology and society?

....
....
....
....
....
....

Quest CHECK-IN

In this lesson, you learned about the characteristics of electromagnetic waves and how polarization works. You also learned about two different models of light. Finally, you learned about the electromagnetic spectrum and the different types of electromagnetic waves, including radio waves, microwaves, infrared rays, ultraviolet rays, x-rays, and gamma rays.

Apply Concepts Think about the properties of visible light and how its path can be changed. How might you move light around an obstacle? What devices might you use in your design?

....
....
....

INTERACTIVITY

Optical Demonstration

Go online to plan your demonstration.

Lights! Camera!
ACTION!

A lighting designer plans how to light a stage or performance space. The designer uses three factors—color, intensity, and motion—to light a show in the most striking and effective way possible.

There are three primary, or basic colors. For pigments, the primary colors are red, yellow, and blue. In lighting, the primary colors are red, green, and blue. When the three primary colors are mixed in equal amounts, a painter ends up with black paint, but a lighting designer creates white light!

Lighting designers use gels to change the colors of stage lights. A gel is a thin sheet of plastic polymer that slides into grooves at the front of the light. Gels come in every color of the rainbow.

Lighting designers can use lots of instruments and a variety of gels to light the stage. By mixing gels, the designer creates new colors. Red and purple gels, used together, make magenta light.

Lighting designers need a good understanding of physics and engineering, as well as dramatic performance, to create effective displays. Lighting designers are called on to illuminate many kinds of spectacles and events. Ice shows, movie sets, political appearances, and concerts are only a few examples of situations in which lighting designers create the right mood and appearance.

▶ **VIDEO**

Explore how lighting designers use and manipulate light to communicate with an audience.

MY CAREER

What kinds of decisions do you think lighting designers have to make? Write down your thoughts and think about whether lighting design might be a good career for you.

A lighting designer shines lights at different angles all around the stage to set a bright and lively mood for this concert.

Guiding Questions

- How are the transmission, reflection, and absorption of light related to the transparency and color of objects?
- What happens to light when it is strikes different types of mirrors?
- What happens to light when it passes through different types of lenses?

Connection

Literacy Evaluate Media

MS-PS4-2

uInvestigate Discover how light is reflected, refracted, and transmitted.

Vocabulary

transparent
translucent
opaque
diffuse reflection
convex
focal point
concave

Academic Vocabulary

compare

Connect It !

✏️ **Shadows are made by different objects in the picture. Label two shadows with the names of the objects that made them.**

Apply Scientific Reasoning Why do some objects make shadows, while others do not?

....

....

....

....

....

Light, Color, and Objects

When people talk about light, they are usually referring to the part of the electromagnetic spectrum that is visible to humans. This light interacts with the world around us to determine what we see and how it appears.

Materials can be classified based on how much light transmits through them. A material that transmits most of the light that strikes it is **transparent**. You can see through a transparent object, such as a window pane or the plastic wrap on a package.

A **translucent** material scatters the light that passes through it. You might be able to see through a translucent material, but the image will look blurred. Waxed paper and gelatin dessert are examples of translucent materials.

A material that reflects or absorbs all of the light that strikes it is called **opaque**. A book, a marshmallow, and a hippopotamus are all opaque—you can't see through them because light does not transmit through them. **Figure 1** shows an example of what happens when light strikes transparent and opaque objects.

INTERACTIVITY

Write about the appearance of your own reflection on several materials.

Reflect Explain why you have a shadow, but a window pane does not.

Shadows

Figure 1 You can see shadows of both the person and the window frame. There is no shadow of the panes of glass in the window because light passes through them.

45

INTERACTIVITY

Observe and describe the behavior of light in various situations.

The Color of Objects

Recall that white light is a mixture of all of the colors in the rainbow. When white light shines on an object, some of the colors of light are reflected and some are absorbed.

The color of an opaque object is the color of light that the object reflects. It absorbs all other colors. Under white light, the soccer ball in **Figure 2** appears blue and red. It reflects blue and red wavelengths of light and absorbs all other colors. Other objects, such as a brown tree trunk, do not appear as basic colors of light. These objects reflect more than one color of light. Brown is a combination of red and green, so a brown object reflects both red and green light, and it absorbs all other colors. If an object appears black, then it absorbs all colors of light. A white object reflects all light.

The color of a transparent or a translucent object is the color of light that passes through it. For example, the color of a clear, green drinking glass is green because green light is the only color of light that passes through it.

☑ READING CHECK **Determine Central Ideas** Why does snow appear white?

....

Light and Color

Figure 2 When light shines on an object, some wavelengths of light are reflected and some are absorbed. ✏ Circle the answers that correctly complete the sentences. The color of an opaque object is the color of light it (absorbs / reflects). If the object (absorbs / reflects) all of the light, the object appears black.

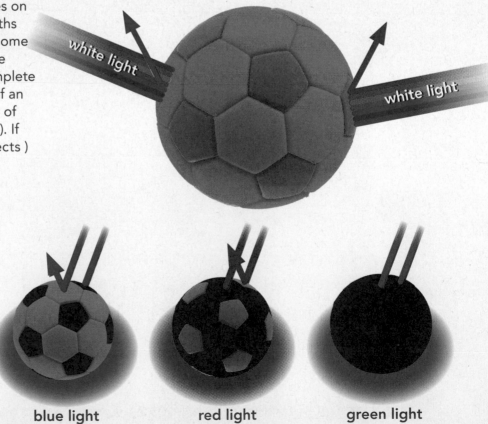

blue light   red light   green light

Color Filters Perhaps you have looked at an object that has a colored light shining on it. You might have noticed that the color of the object looks different than it does when white light shines on it. The color of the light might come from white light shining through a colored filter—a tinted piece of glass or plastic. A red filter, for example, transmits only red light. When light shines through a red filter onto an object, any part of the object that is red, looks red. Any other color looks black. **Figure 3** shows several different color filters and what happens when white light shines on them.

Color filters are often used in photography and movies. They are part of the special effects that create different moods for scenes. Use what you know about filters to complete the activity in **Figure 3**.

INTERACTIVITY

Explore how color filters affect the appearance of different objects.

Literacy Connection

Evaluate Media Describe an image you've seen with a filter on it, and write about how the filter altered the image.

....
....
....
....

Photography and Color Filters
Figure 3 ✏️ Color filters can be used in photography to bring out certain colors or create dramatic moods. For each of the inset images, write the color of the filter that produced the altered images.

Investigate Discover how light is reflected, refracted, and transmitted.

Reflecting Light

You have seen that sometimes light is transmitted through materials. Like other electromagnetic radiation, light can also be reflected. The reflection of light occurs when parallel rays of light bounce off a surface. Reflected light is how you see your image in a mirror, but reflected light is also why you see a distorted image or no image at all in the surface of rippling water on a lake. The difference lies in whether the light undergoes regular reflection or diffuse reflection.

Regular reflection occurs when parallel rays of light hit a smooth surface. As shown in **Figure 4**, the trees are reflected because light hits the smooth surface of the water, and the rays all reflect at the same angle. As a result, the reflection is a clear image.

In **diffuse reflection**, parallel rays of light hit an uneven surface. The angle at which each ray hits the surface equals the angle at which it reflects. The rays, however, don't bounce off in the same direction because the light rays hit different parts of the surface at different angles. **Figure 4** shows why light undergoes diffuse reflection when it hits choppy water on a lake.

Regular and Diffuse Reflection

Figure 4 Light reflects off the surface of water.

✏️ For each type of reflection, circle the terms that correctly complete the sentence.

You (can / cannot) see an image in the still water because the light undergoes (regular / diffuse) reflection.

You (can / cannot) see an image in the choppy water because the light undergoes (regular / diffuse) reflection.

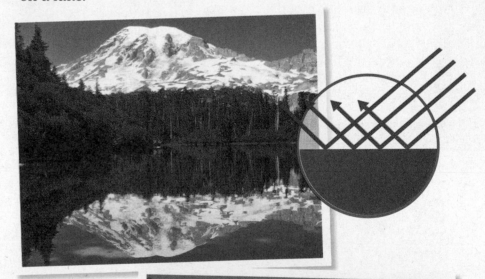

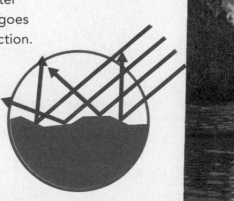

Mirror Images

The most common way to form a clear image using reflected light is with a mirror. There are three different types of mirrors—plane, convex, and concave. The types of mirrors are distinguished by the shape of the surface of the mirror.

The mirror you have hanging on a wall in your home probably is a flat mirror, also known as a plane mirror. The image you see in the mirror is called a virtual image, which is an image that forms where light seems to come from. **Figure 5** shows an example of a virtual image in a plane mirror. This image is upright and the same size as the object that formed the image, but the right and left sides of the image are reversed.

Convex Mirrors

To visualize a convex mirror, think about a metal bowl. A **convex** mirror is like the outside of the bowl because it is a mirror with a surface that curves outward. If you look at an image in the outside of the bowl, it is smaller than the image in a plane mirror. **Figure 6** shows an example of an image in a convex mirror. To understand how these images form, look at the optical axis and the focal point of the mirror. The optical axis is an imaginary line that divides a mirror in half. The **focal point** is the location at which rays parallel to the optical axis reflect and meet. The light reflects off the curved surface such that the image appears to come from a focal point behind the mirror.

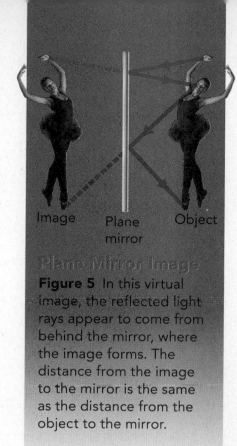

Image   Plane   Object
         mirror

Plane Mirror Image

Figure 5 In this virtual image, the reflected light rays appear to come from behind the mirror, where the image forms. The distance from the image to the mirror is the same as the distance from the object to the mirror.

Convex Mirror Image

Figure 6 Most rear-view mirrors are convex. Light rays bend when they hit the surface of the mirror in such a way that the object appears smaller than it is.

Optical axis

Focal point

49

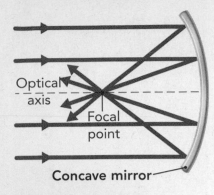

Optical axis

Focal point

Concave mirror

Mirror Images

Figure 7 The images formed by mirrors depend upon the shape of the mirror. Examine the diagram, and then identify the type of image in each example.

The object is located farther from the mirror than the focal point is. It forms a .... image.

The object is located between the mirror and the focal point. It forms a .... image.

Concave Mirrors Just as a convex mirror is like the outside of a shiny bowl, a concave mirror is like the inside of the bowl. The surface of a concave mirror curves inward. **Figure 7** shows that the focal point of a concave mirror is on the reflecting side of the mirror. The image that forms from a concave mirror depends on whether the object is between the focal point and the mirror or farther away from the mirror than the focal point. If the object is farther from the mirror than the focal point is, then reflected light rays cross past one another, and the image is inverted. This image is called a real image. If the object is between the focal point and the mirror, then the image is not inverted and is larger than the actual object. This image is a virtual image.

✓ **READING CHECK** **Classify** If a mirrored image is inverted, what type of image is it?

....

Fun with Mirrors

In a fun house, mirrors are often used to change the appearance of objects.

Develop Models ✏ Suppose you want to use a mirror to make a door look smaller and rounder. In the space below, draw the mirror and the door, along with the focal point. Label the mirror with the type of mirror it is.

Lenses

Light not only reflects, as it does with a mirror, but it also bends, or refracts. A lens is a curved piece of transparent material that refracts light. Every time you look through a telescope, a microscope, or a pair of eyeglasses, you are looking through a lens. Just like a mirror, a lens is either convex or concave, based on its shape.

Convex Lenses Look at **Figure 8** to see what convex lenses look like, how they refract light, and what type of image is produced. You can see that convex lenses are thicker in the middle and thinner at the edges. As light passes through the lens, it refracts toward the center of the lens. The more curved the lens is, the more the light refracts.

A convex lens can produce either a virtual image or a real image depending on where the object is located relative to the focal point of the lens. If the object is between the lens and the focal point, then a virtual image forms. This image is larger than the actual object. You may have observed this when using a magnifying glass. If the object is farther away from the lens than the focal point is, then a real image forms. This image can be larger, smaller, or the same size as the object.

Does this description of a convex lens sound familiar? Compare a convex lens and a concave mirror. Both a convex lens and a concave mirror focus light, and the type of image formed depends on the location of the object compared to the location of the focal point.

▶ VIDEO

Explore the effects of different lenses and filters in cameras.

Academic Vocabulary

How does comparing items differ from contrasting them?

....

....

....

....

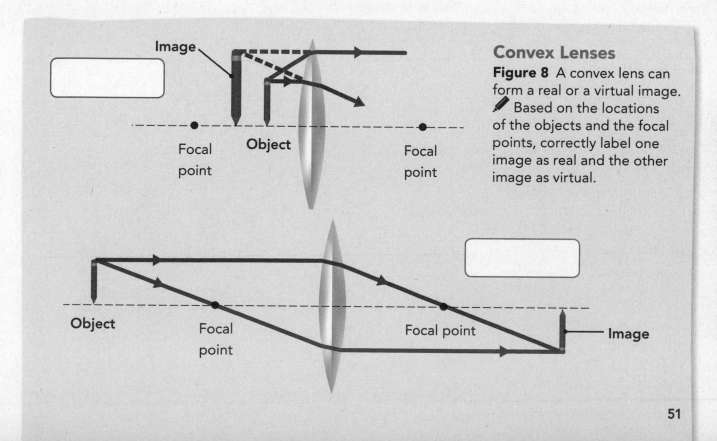

Convex Lenses

Figure 8 A convex lens can form a real or a virtual image.
🖊 Based on the locations of the objects and the focal points, correctly label one image as real and the other image as virtual.

Predict the behavior of light rays as they encounter different objects and substances.

Concave Lenses

Concave lenses are thinner at the center than they are at the edges. When light rays travel through the lens, the rays are bent away from the optical axis, so the rays never meet. Because the rays never meet, concave lenses form only virtual images, and these images are upright and smaller than the objects. **Figure 9** shows how concave lenses form images.

☑ **READING CHECK** **Compare and Contrast** In what ways is a convex lens like a concave mirror? In what ways are they different?

....

....

....

....

Concave Lenses

Figure 9 When looking through a concave lens, a virtual image forms which is always smaller than the object itself. ✎ After examining the diagrams, circle the photo in which the image is formed by using a concave lens.

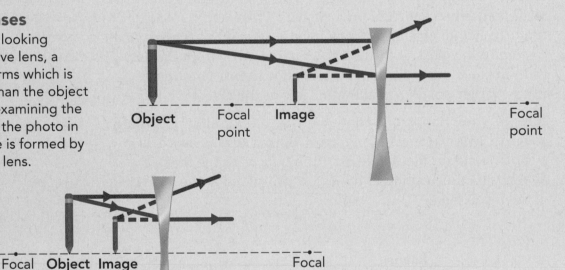

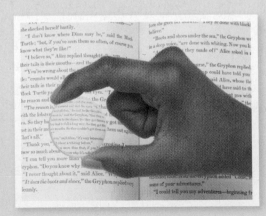

MS-PS4-2

1. Classify What kind of material transmits some light, making objects behind it appear blurry?

....

....

....

2. Identify A bird runs into the window of a building because it sees the reflection of the sky in the window. The sky does not appear distorted in this window. What type of mirror or lens is the window acting as? Explain your answer.

....

....

....

....

3. Apply Scientific Reasoning When a person is nearsighted, an eyeglass lens is needed to bend light entering the eye away from the optical axis. What type of lens will do this?

....

....

4. Cause and Effect Why might some rear-view mirrors in a car state, "Objects are closer than they appear"?

....

....

....

....

....

5. Construct Explanations Suppose a movie director is filming on a set that should look like a hot desert. He wants the scene to appear warmer, such that the red and yellow tones are the most apparent. What color filters should he use? What color will the blue sky appear when he uses those filters, and why?

....

....

....

....

....

....

....

Quest CHECK-IN

HANDS-ON LAB

An Optimal Optical Solution

In this lesson, you observed how light behaves when it encounters transparent, translucent, and opaque objects. You saw how the color of light or filters affects the color of objects. You also discovered the ways that light can reflect from mirrors or refract through lenses.

Go online to download the lab worksheet. Build and test your optical security system.

How might you apply this knowledge to choose the objects and their placement in your quest?

....

....

....

....

☑TOPIC 1 Review and Assess

1 Wave Properties

MS-PS4-1

1. Which of the following is a property of a mechanical wave?
   A. amplitude
   B. weight
   C. incidence
   D. color

2. The sound wave frequency of an F-sharp in music is 370 Hz, and its wavelength is 0.93 m. What is the wave's speed?
   A. 34.4 m/s
   B. 397.9 m/s
   C. 344.1 m/s
   D. 300,000 km/s

3. Which statement about the speed of sound is correct?
   A. Sound travels faster through water than air.
   B. Sound travels at the same speed through water and air.
   C. Sound travels faster through space than air.
   D. Sound travels at the same speed through space and air.

4. If the amplitude or frequency of a wave increases, the energy of the wave ....

5. Construct Explanations It's been said that you can estimate how far away a lightning bolt is by counting the number of seconds that elapse between seeing the flash and hearing the thunderclap, and then dividing that number by five to get a distance in miles. In terms of the physics of light and sound waves, does this method make sense?

....

....

....

....

....

....

....

2 Wave Interactions

MS-PS4-2

6. Refraction is the bending of waves that occurs due to a change in
   A. speed.
   B. frequency.
   C. height.
   D. amplitude.

7. Which of the following pairs of terms describes the two different wave interactions depicted below?

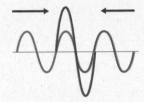 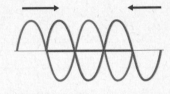

   A. constructive and destructive interference
   B. moving and standing waves
   C. mechanical and electromagnetic waves
   D. sound waves and light waves

8. When a ray of light strikes a surface, it can be
   ...., ...,
   or ....

9. Construct Arguments Why is it important for engineers to understand the natural frequency of vibrations in building materials when planning to build a bridge in an area with high winds or frequent earthquakes?

....

....

....

....

....

....

....

3 Sound Waves

MS-PS4-2

10. When a sound wave is absorbed by an object,
   A. it quickly gains energy.
   B. it quickly loses energy.
   C. it slowly gains energy.
   D. its energy does not change.

11. Analyze Properties How do stiffness, density, and temperature affect sound waves?

....

....

....

....

....

4 Electromagnetic Waves

MS-PS4-2

12. Which electromagnetic wave type has the highest frequency?
   A. visible light
   B. infrared rays
   C. gamma rays
   D. microwaves

13. Of all of the colors in the visible part of the electromagnetic spectrum, red light has the lowest frequency, the .... wavelength, and the .... energy.

14. Use Models Describe how you could use a simple rope to teach someone about the different waves along the electromagnetic spectrum.

....

....

....

....

....

5 Electromagnetic Radiation

MS-PS4-2

15. Which statement is correct?
   A. A red apple reflects green light.
   B. A blue ball absorbs blue light.
   C. A green leaf reflects green light.
   D. A black shirt reflects all colors of light.

16. What happens when light rays encounter a concave lens?
   A. The light rays are reflected back.
   B. The light rays travel through the lens and refract away from the center of the lens.
   C. The light rays travel through the lens and refract toward the center of the lens.
   D. The light rays travel through the lens without bending.

17. When an object is located between a concave mirror and the focal point, a .... image is produced.

18. Develop Models ✏ Draw a model to show what happens to light when it meets a convex mirror.

MS-PS4-1, MS-PS4-2

Evidence-Based Assessment

Bianca is helping the theater director at her school with lighting, sound, and set design for a school play. She will be choosing the materials that will be used on stage and on the walls of the theater. After she reads the script and makes observations inside the theater, she makes the following list of the factors to consider in her design.

- The echoes throughout the theater need to be reduced.

- The set should not reflect too much light into the audience's eyes.

- The only lights available are white, purple, and yellow. The filters available are red and blue.

- The blue sky on the set should appear black for Act 2.

Bianca draws a detailed illustration of her plan to show the theater director. She labels it with the materials she plans to use.

1. **Apply Scientific Reasoning** Bianca plans to shine a few spotlights on the sky for Act 2 and use a filter to change the color. Which filter should Bianca use on the white light to make the blue sky appear black?
   A. a red filter
   B. a blue filter
   C. a white filter
   D. no filter at all

2. **Identify Criteria** Which of the following considerations does Bianca need to take into account as she works on the set and lighting design? Select all that apply.
   ☐ Two different sets are needed for Act 2.
   ☐ The set materials should not be too shiny or glossy.
   ☐ Only the colors white, purple, and yellow can be used to paint the sets.
   ☐ The walls have hard surfaces that reflect sound waves.
   ☐ Only the white lights can be used for Act 2.

3. **Use Models** Based on Bianca's illustration, did she choose the appropriate material on the walls for reducing echoes? Why or why not?

   ....
   ....
   ....
   ....

4. **Develop Models** As sound waves travel away from the speaker, their amplitudes and energy decrease. Where will the sound be the most quiet? If you were to move the speaker, where would you place it and why?

   ....
   ....
   ....
   ....
   ....
   ....

5. **Provide Critique** Based on Bianca's criteria and model, which materials would you change on stage? Explain your reasoning.

   ....
   ....
   ....
   ....
   ....
   ....
   ....
   ....
   ....

Quest FINDINGS

Complete the Quest!

Phenomenon Reflect on your demonstration and answer questions about modifying and improving your design. List some other kinds of jobs that may require a good knowledge of light and its behavior.

Apply Concepts You've seen how light can bend and move. How might a grocery store manager use the properties of light and set up objects to make sure the entire store can be visible from one location without using cameras?

....
....
....
....

👆 **INTERACTIVITY**

Reflect on Your Demonstration

Making Waves

How can you use a **model** to demonstrate what happens when **waves interact** with barriers or other waves?

Background

Phenomenon A wave breaker is a large wall made of rocks or concrete objects that extends into the ocean. Breakers often are built near beaches to make the water calmer for swimmers. These barriers help to diminish the force of incoming waves by scattering them and interfering with their movements.

In this lab, you will model the behavior of water waves and explain how the waves interact with each other and with objects in their paths. You will then decide on the best method and materials for diminishing waves.

(per group)

- water
- plastic dropper
- metric ruler
- paper towels
- modeling clay
- plastic knife
- cork or other small floating object
- ripple tank (aluminum foil lasagna pan with mirror on the bottom)

Be sure to follow all safety guidelines provided by your teacher.

This rock barrier helps to block big waves and make the beach more enjoyable for swimmers.

Design an Investigation

☐ One way to generate waves is to squeeze drops of water from an eyedropper into a pan of water. How can you use the dropper to control how forceful the waves are?

....

....

....

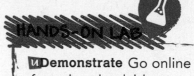

HANDS-ON LAB

ИDemonstrate Go online for a downloadable worksheet of this lab.

☐ What questions will you explore in your investigation? Some questions to explore include:

- What happens when waves hit a solid surface?

- What happens when waves travel through a gap between two solid objects?

- How does a floating object react to waves?

- What happens when one wave meets another wave?

☐ Record any additional questions you hope to answer in your investigation.

....

....

....

☐ Design an experiment to show how waves behave when they interact with different objects or with each other. Write out a procedure. Then decide what information to record and design a data table to record your observations.

Procedure

Data

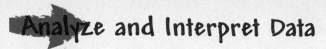

Analyze and Interpret Data

1. **Identify** Are the waves in water mechanical waves or electromagnetic waves? How do you know?

....

....

....

2. **Make Observations** In what situations did you observe waves interfering with one another? How did it affect the amplitude of the waves?

....

....

....

....

....

3. **Evaluate Your Tests** Repetition is when you repeat a step of the procedure a few times to see if you get the same results. Did you use repetition in your experiment? Why or why not?

....

....

....

4. **Relate Structure and Function** Which material and set-up was best for diminishing waves? Which was the worst? What evidence led you to these conclusions?

....

....

....

....

....

5. **Provide Critique** Share your results with members of another group. What did they do differently? In what ways would you suggest that the other group members revise their procedure?

....

....

....

....

TOPIC

2

Information Technologies

LESSON 1
Electric Circuits
uInvestigate Lab: Electric Current
and Voltage

uEngineer It! STEM **A Life-Saving
Mistake**

LESSON 2
Signals
uInvestigate Lab: Constructing a
Simple Computer Circuit

LESSON 3
Communication and
Technology
uInvestigate Lab: Let the Music Play

NGSS PERFORMANCE EXPECTATIONS

MS-PS4-3 Integrate qualitative scientific and
technical information to support the claim that
digitized signals are a more reliable way to encode
and transmit information than analog signals.

What do these
tiny circuits do?

HANDS-ON LAB

uConnect Consider ways to represent
the terms *continuous* and *discrete*.

GO ONLINE
to access your
digital course

▶ VIDEO

👆 INTERACTIVITY

🧪 VIRTUAL LAB

☑ ASSESSMENT

📖 eTEXT

🧪 HANDS-ON LABS

The Essential Question

Why are digital signals a reliable way to produce, store, and transmit information?

Circuit boards are found in all kinds of electronics devices, from toasters to televisions. How is information transmitted through these boards?

....

....

....

....

....

Quest KICKOFF

What is the best way to record sound for my scenario?

NBC LEARN ▶ VIDEO

STEM ▷ **Phenomenon** Sound engineers work on all kinds of audio recordings, from television shows and movies to music albums. If you wanted to record people's voices and manipulate them to use as sound effects, then how would you do it? In this Quest activity, you will identify the most reliable way to encode and transmit an audio recording. You will explore differences between analog and digital technologies with a hands-on lab and digital activities. By applying what you have learned, you will create a multimedia display that communicates your findings.

After watching the video, which looks at how an audio engineer records sound, describe how attending a live concert is different than listening to an album recorded in a studio.

....

....

....

....

....

....

....

👆 **INTERACTIVITY**

Testing, Testing . . . 1, 2, 3

MS-PS4-3 Integrate qualitative scientific and technical information to support the claim that digitized signals are a more reliable way to encode and transmit information than analog signals.

Quest CHECK-IN

IN LESSON 1

STEM ▷ How does a microphone convert sound waves into electrical signals? Design and build a model of a microphone to learn how.

🧪

HANDS-ON LAB

Constructing a Microphone

Quest CHECK-IN

IN LESSON 2

How has recording technology changed? Consider the advantages and disadvantages of analog and digital recording technologies.

👆 **INTERACTIVITY**

Analog and Digital Recordings

Microphones are just one of the many kinds of technology used to record sound.

Quest CHECK-IN

IN LESSON 3

What type of recording technology would best suit your scenario? Design a multimedia presentation that communicates your choices and reasons.

 INTERACTIVITY

Evaluate Recording Technologies

Quest FINDINGS

Complete the Quest!

Reflect on your work and identify fields or careers that require knowledge of analog and digital signals.

 INTERACTIVITY

Reflect on Your Recording Method

1 Electric Circuits

Guiding Questions

- What are the components of a circuit?
- How does Ohm's law apply to circuits?
- What is the difference between a series circuit and a parallel circuit?

Connections

Literacy Determine Central Ideas

Math Use Proportional Relationships

MS-PS4-3

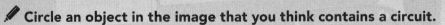

HANDS-ON LAB

uInvestigate Explore Ohm's law in action with your own circuit.

Vocabulary

electrical circuit
voltage
resistance
Ohm's law
series circuit
parallel circuit

Academic Vocabulary

diameter

✏ **Circle an object in the image that you think contains a circuit.**

Analyze Systems What provides the energy for the circuit?

....

....

Explain Phenomena Describe any transformations of energy that occur in the circuit.

....

....

Parts of a Circuit

The wall clock in **Figure 1** is part of an electrical circuit. An **electrical circuit** is a complete, unbroken path that electric charges can flow through.

A circuit consists of a few basic parts: a source of electrical energy, conducting wires, and a device that runs on the electrical energy. In a wall clock batteries are the source of electrical energy. Conducting wires connect the batteries to a motor attached to the clock's arms. The motor runs on electrical energy—converting the batteries' energy to the clock's motions. Circuits sometimes also contain switches. When a switch is closed, charges can flow through the circuit. When a switch is open, the circuit is broken and charges cannot flow. A light switch in your home is used to open and close the circuit that sends electrical energy from a power plant to your light bulb.

Even though energy in circuits is used to power devices, the energy is always conserved. The electrical energy does not get used up—instead, it is transformed from one form to another. For example, in a table lamp, the electrical energy is transformed into light and heat.

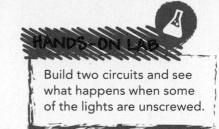

HANDS-ON LAB

Build two circuits and see what happens when some of the lights are unscrewed.

Electric Circuits in a Home

Figure 1 Many devices in a typical home contain circuits and use electricity.

Potential Energy

Figure 2 Objects at higher positions have greater potential energy per unit of mass. Similarly, a battery with a higher voltage has greater electrical potential energy per charge.

Develop Models ✏️ Draw an X on the water slide where a person would have the greatest gravitational potential energy per unit of mass. Draw an X on the circuit where it has the greatest electric potential energy per charge.

Literacy Connection

Determine Central Ideas What does voltage measure?

....

....

....

....

....

Voltage Electric current flows through a circuit because of differences in electric potential energy in the electric charges. In circuits, it is helpful to think about the electric potential energy per charge, or electric potential, at different points in a circuit. **Voltage** is the difference in electric potential energy per charge between two points in a circuit. So, voltage is the difference in electric potential. Voltage is measured in volts (V).

A typical battery has two ends. One end has a higher electric potential than the other. The end with higher electric potential is called the positive end, and the end with lower electric potential is the negative end. The difference in electric potential is the battery's voltage. For example, the positive end of a 12-volt battery has an electric potential 12 volts higher than the negative end. When the battery is connected within a circuit, this voltage causes current to flow. The current moves from the positive end through the circuit and back to the negative end. The current flows naturally, much like water on a water slide (**Figure 2**).

As the current flows through the circuit, the electric potential energy is converted to other forms of energy. As a result, the electric potential drops as the charges move through the circuit. When the charges reach the battery, they need to regain potential energy if the current is going to continue. The battery supplies the charges with energy by converting chemical energy (from chemicals within the battery) to electrical energy.

The directions of current and voltage were originally defined for positive charges. It was later discovered that negatively-charged electrons flow through a wire circuit. It can be confusing, but remember that what we call electric current goes in the opposite direction of the actual flow of electrons.

Resistance

Resistance Objects that run on electricity act as resistance to the flow of current. Resistance is a measure of how difficult it is for current to flow through an object. It takes more energy for charges to move through objects with higher resistance. Therefore, there is a greater drop in electric potential as the current flows through the circuit. Objects that provide resistance are called resistors. A light bulb, for example, acts as a resistor (**Figure 3**).

The resistance of an object depends on its diameter, length, temperature, and material. Objects with a smaller diameter and longer length are more difficult to flow through. In the same way, it is more difficult to sip a drink through a narrow and long straw than a wide and short straw. Current also flows more easily through an object when it is cold than when it is hot. Warmer particles vibrate more and obstruct the flow of current. Current also flows more easily through materials that are good conductors. The conductors have electrons that are more loosely bound, so the charges can move more easily.

☑ **READING CHECK** **Summarize** What kind of device in a circuit supplies voltage? What kind of device acts as a resistor?

....

....

....

....

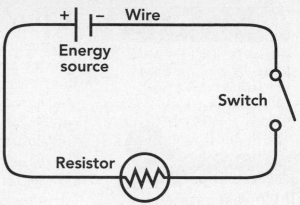

Potential Energy

Figure 3 The diagrams show a circuit with a battery, conducting wires, a switch, and a light bulb.

Academic Vocabulary

The diameter of a circle is the distance across the center. This is the full width of the circle. How would you describe the diameter of a round wire?

....

....

....

Drawing Circuit Diagrams

As shown in **Figure 3**, symbols are used in a diagram to show the parts of a circuit.

1. **Develop Models** 🖊 In the space provided, draw what the circuit in **Figure 3** would look like if another battery and another light bulb were added.

2. **Predict** Will the total resistance in the circuit increase or decrease when more light bulbs are added? Explain.

....

....

....

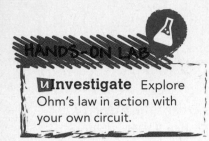

HANDS-ON LAB

Investigate Explore Ohm's law in action with your own circuit.

Ohm's Law

About 200 years ago, scientist Georg Ohm experimented with electric circuits. He measured the resistance of a conductor and varied the voltage to find the relationship between resistance and voltage. He found that changing the voltage in the circuit changes the current but does not change the resistance of the conductor. When voltage increases, current increases but resistance does not change. Ohm came up with a law for this relationship. **Ohm's law** states that resistance in a circuit is equal to voltage divided by current.

$$\text{Resistance} = \frac{\text{Voltage}}{\text{Current}}$$

Resistance is measured in ohms (Ω). This means that one ohm of resistance is equal to one volt (V) divided by one amp (A). If you increase voltage without changing resistance, then current must increase as well.

Solving this equation for voltage, you obtain:

$$\text{Voltage} = \text{Current} \times \text{Resistance}$$

If you increase the resistance of a circuit without changing the voltage, then the current must decrease.

Math Toolbox

Applying Ohm's Law

A stereo converts electrical energy into sound energy. The stereo is plugged into a wall outlet. The voltage is supplied by a power plant, and the current is carried through electrical wires to the stereo.

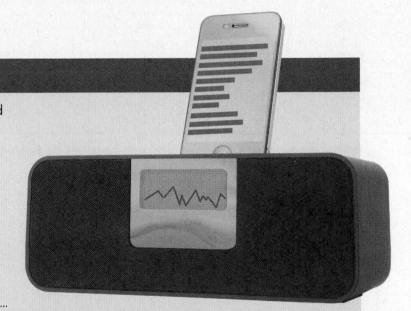

1. **Use Proportional Relationships** When you turn up the volume on a stereo, the voltage increases. Assuming the resistance of the stereo remains the same, what happens to the current?

   ....

2. **Use Equations** Suppose you turn up the volume on a stereo so that the voltage increases to 110 V while the resistance remains at 55 Ω. Calculate the current after this voltage increase.

   ....

   ....

Series and Parallel Circuits

Different situations may call for different types of circuits. Suppose a factory uses multiple machines in an assembly line to recycle glass bottles. If the glass-melting machine breaks down but the bottles keep moving, there could be a major safety hazard as the bottles pile up! To prevent this problem, the machines can be wired so that if one machine breaks, then the circuit is broken and all other machines stop working as well. This is called a series circuit.

Series Circuits In a <mark>series circuit</mark>, all parts of the circuit are connected one after another along one path (**Figure 4**). There are advantages to setting up a circuit this way, as in the example of the recycling factory. However, it can sometimes be a disadvantage. The more devices you add to the circuit, the more resistance there is. As you learned with Ohm's law, if voltage remains the same and resistance increases, then current decreases. Adding more light bulbs to a string of lights causes them to shine less brightly. The circuit would have more resistance and the current would decrease, causing the bulbs to appear dimmer.

Write About It Give one example of a situation in your life in which a series circuit is an advantage, and another example in which it could be a disadvantage.

Correcting Circuit Diagrams

Figure 4 An electrical engineer draws a circuit diagram of a series circuit that includes three resistors, two batteries, and a switch. Find the engineer's mistake, and mark the drawing with your correction.

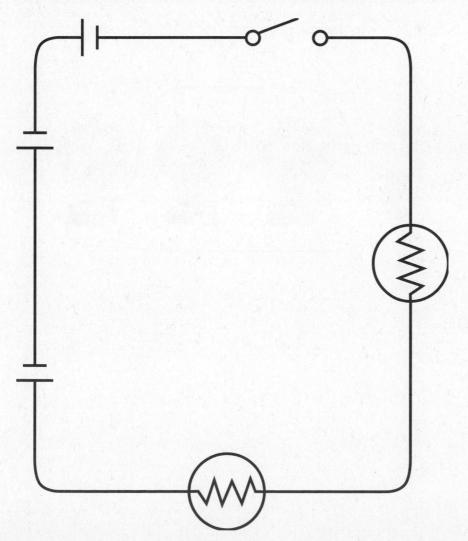

INTERACTIVITY

Review the parts of a circuit and fix a set of broken lights.

Parallel Circuits

In other situations, you may want each device in a circuit to be wired so that if one device breaks, the others still work. For instance, when one overhead light burns out in the kitchen, you don't expect the other lights to go out, leaving you in the dark. In situations like this, you should use a **parallel circuit**, in which different parts of the circuit are on separate branches. As shown in **Figure 5**, there are several paths for the current to take in a parallel circuit.

Surprisingly, adding resistors in parallel to the circuit actually causes resistance to decrease. How is this possible? Adding a branch opens up another path for current to flow. This is similar to adding another pipe for water to flow through. Therefore, resistance in the circuit decreases and current increases. However, the additional current flows down the new path, so it does not affect the other devices. If a string of lights is set up along a parallel circuit, then each new bulb you add will glow as brightly as those originally on the strand.

☑ READING CHECK **Determine Central Ideas** Describe the main difference between a series circuit and a parallel circuit.

....

....

Light Bulbs in Parallel

Figure 5 The circuit diagram shows three light bulbs in parallel.

1. **Cause and Effect** What happens to the other two light bulbs when one light bulb goes out? Explain.

....

....

....

....

....

....

2. **Develop Models** ✏
Draw the circuit again, adding one switch to each branch so that the bulbs can be controlled separately.

At the Boardwalk

Figure 6 🖍 Many activities at the boardwalk involve circuits. Circle the places where circuits would be.

Construct Explanations Why do you think five of the last lights on the Ferris wheel have gone out?

....

....

....

1. **Identify** What are the three main parts that must be present to make up a circuit?

....

....

....

2. **Define** How is voltage related to electric potential energy?

....

....

....

....

3. **Develop Models** ✏ Draw a series circuit diagram that contains a battery, a switch, and three resistors. Label the parts of the circuit.

4. **Use Information** A long, narrow resistor is placed in a series circuit along with a short, wide resistor made of the same material. Which will have a greater electric potential drop across it? Explain your reasoning.

....

....

....

....

....

5. **Cause and Effect** Suppose you construct a parallel circuit consisting of a battery, a switch, and four light bulbs. One of the light bulbs goes out. What happens to the brightness of the remaining bulbs? Explain.

....

....

....

....

....

....

Quest CHECK-IN

You have discovered the meaning of voltage and resistance and how they relate to current as described by Ohm's law. You've also read about the different parts of a circuit and how to connect them in series or in parallel.

Communicate How might your understanding of circuits help you decide what type of recording device to use?

....

....

....

HANDS-ON LAB

Constructing a Microphone

Go online to download the lab worksheet. Develop and use a model that shows how a simple microphone converts sound waves into electrical signals.

MS-PS4-3

A LIFE-SAVING Mistake

INTERACTIVITY

Explore what makes up a pacemaker and how it works.

How do you create a tiny device that saves hundreds of thousands of lives? You engineer it! The story of Wilson Greatbatch shows us how.

The Challenge: To develop the first successful cardiac pacemaker.

Phenomenon In 1956, Greatbatch was working at the University of Buffalo, in New York, as an assistant professor in electrical engineering. He was building an electronic device to record the heart rhythms of cardiac patients. While tinkering with the circuitry, he made a mistake and put a resistor into the circuit that was the wrong size.

When Greatbatch added the resistor, he did not get the outcome he expected. The circuit periodically buzzed with electrical pulses that reminded the engineer of a human heartbeat.

Greatbatch's error turned out to be a happy accident. He realized that the device could help cardiac patients whose hearts beat irregularly. He used the idea to develop the first successful pacemaker, a device that delivers small electrical shocks to the heart muscle to keep it beating regularly and pumping blood normally.

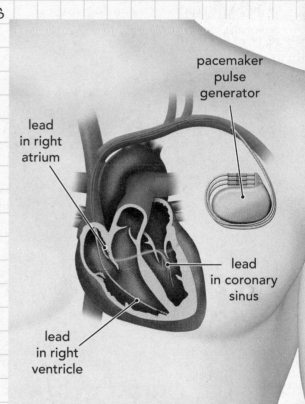

pacemaker pulse generator

lead in right atrium

lead in coronary sinus

lead in right ventricle

A pacemaker uses a pulse generator implanted below a patient's skin to send electric pulses to the heart. The pulses travel through wires called leads.

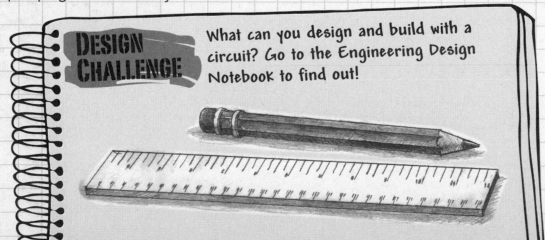

DESIGN CHALLENGE What can you design and build with a circuit? Go to the Engineering Design Notebook to find out!

Guiding Questions

- How is information sent as signals?
- What are digital and analog signals?
- How are signals transmitted?

Connections

Literacy Summarize Text

Math Draw Comparative Inferences

MS-PS4-3

HANDS-ON LAB

uInvestigate Explore how analog signals can be converted to digital information.

Vocabulary

wave pulse
electronic signal
electromagnetic
  signal
digital signal
analog signal
pixel

Academic Vocabulary

transmission

Connect It!

✏ **Circle the visual signal that is being used to communicate information.**

Construct Explanations Why do you think hand signals are useful for communicating with a dog?

....

....

....

....

....

Signals and Information

An electric circuit can be used to power a device like a light bulb. However, circuits can also be used to send information. Think about a doorbell, which is usually a circuit. When someone presses a button outside a door, the circuit is complete and the electricity powers a bell that chimes. If you understand the meaning of the chime (a signal that someone is at the door), then you can respond by going to the door. For any signal to be understood, there needs to be agreement between the sender and the receiver about what the signal means. In some cases, the signal can be simple, such as a doorbell or basic hand signals, like the one the pet owner is using in **Figure 1**. Others are more complex. For example, you are reading a specific sequence of letters and spaces on this page to learn about signals.

For much of the 1800s, people communicated with each other over great distances using electrical signals. Samuel Morse patented a version of the electrical telegraph in 1837, and by the Civil War in 1861, there were telegraph lines that carried Morse code from one side of the United States to the other.

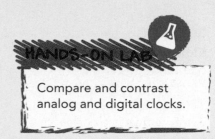

HANDS-ON LAB

Compare and contrast analog and digital clocks.

Signaling

Figure 1 A human can teach a dog to respond to visual signals.

Morse Code

Figure 2 In Morse code, combinations of short (dot) and long (dash) wave pulses are sent and each combination is translated into a letter.

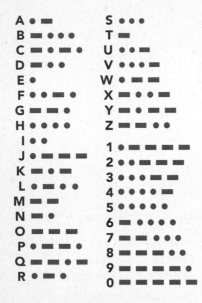

Electronic Signals

Electronic Signals An electrical telegraph is used to send Morse code as an electronic signal, information that is sent as a pattern in a controlled flow of current through a circuit. The telegraph turns the current on and off as the operator taps a device to close and open the circuit, as shown in **Figure 2**. In Morse code, combinations of short (dot) and long (dash) wave pulses stand for the letters of the alphabet and punctuation marks. A wave pulse is a pulse of energy that travels through the circuit when it is closed. In Morse code, the letter *A* is sent and received as "•—", *B* is "—•••", and so on. This code can be used to send messages, but it is very slow.

Electronic signaling became more useful and widespread when inventors developed ways to transmit information without translating them into code. In 1876, Alexander Graham Bell patented the first telephone. In Bell's telephone, two people spoke into devices that were part of the same circuit. A microphone converted soundwaves in the in air—a caller's voice—into electronic signals that would be carried to the receiver somewhere else. At the time, switchboard operators manually connected two telephones into the same circuit. Eventually, switchboards became fully automated.

Model It!

Be a Telegraph Operator

1. **Interpret Visuals** Use the Morse code chart in **Figure 2** to decode the following four lines of code.

   •——   ••••   •—   —   ....

   ••   •••   ....

   ••—•   ———   •—•   ....

   •—••   ••—   —•   —•—•   ••••   ....

2. **Use a Model** ✏ Use Morse code to provide an answer to the message you decoded.

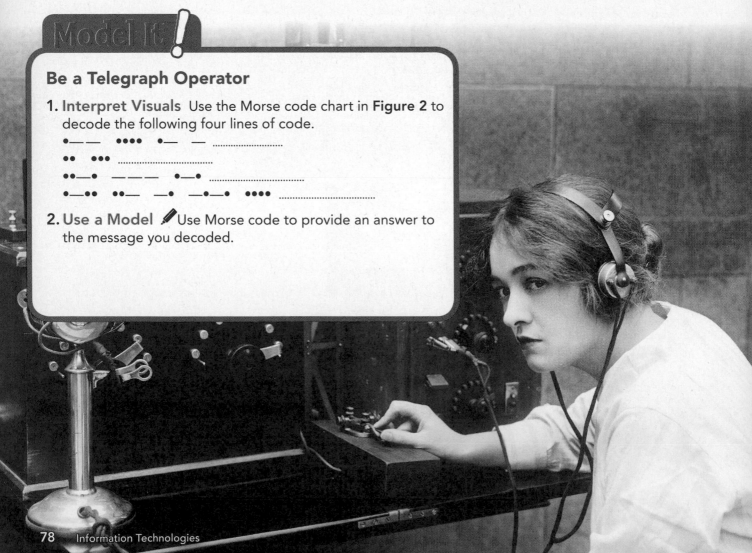

Electronic Signals	Electromagnetic Signals

Electromagnetic Signals

Information sent as patterns of electromagnetic waves such as visible light, infrared waves, microwaves, and radio waves are **electromagnetic signals**. Modern information technologies use a combination of electronic and electromagnetic signals. In 1895, the first radio station transmitted radio wave signals between two points without using an electrical circuit. This launched wireless forms of communication that allowed messages to be transmitted across the globe. Wireless technologies, such as the ones shown in **Figure 3**, now dominate the telecommunications industry. Electromagnetic signals travel at the speed of light, which is much faster than the speed at which current flows through a circuit.

Different types of electromagnetic signals are used for different purposes. Modern mobile phones communicate using microwaves, which are in the ultra-high frequency (UHF) band of the electromagnetic spectrum. Submarines communicate underwater with extremely low frequency (ELF) waves. Optical fibers use visible and infrared light to transmit large amounts of information.

☑ **READING CHECK** **Determine Central Ideas** What is an electronic signal?

....

....

From Wired to Wireless

Figure 3 The transition from wired to wireless telecommunications has allowed people to communicate and share information with each other with greater convenience, speed, and quality.

Compare and Contrast
✏ Complete the table to compare and contrast electronic and electromagnetic signals.

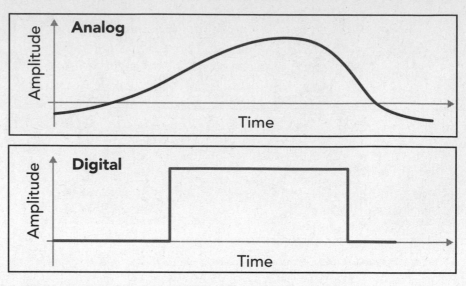

▶ **VIDEO**

Compare analog sound recording devices to newer digital technologies.

Literacy Connection

Summarize Texts
Underline the sentences that summarize the differences between analog and digital signals.

Analog and Digital Signals

Electronic and electromagnetic signals can carry information from one place to another in two different ways: as analog signals or as digital signals. Both analog and digital signals have strengths and weaknesses, but the power and flexibility of digital signals have made them the foundation of modern information technologies.

Analog Signals An analog signal allows for a continuous record of some kind of action (**Figure 4**). For example, when seismic waves from an earthquake cause the ground to move, a seismograph records that continuous motion as an analog signal. The advantage of analog signals is that they provide the highest resolution of an action by recording it continuously. But analog signals can be difficult to record. The signals processed by a seismograph must be recorded with ink on paper as a seismogram. Other examples of analog signals are the recordings of music on vinyl records. You can slow down a record and still hear continuous music. However, vinyl records scratch and warp very easily. Analog media also take up a lot of space, compared to digital media.

Digital Signals A digital signal allows for a record of numerical values of an action at a set of continuous time intervals (**Figure 4**). This results in a series of numbers. For example, a digital seismometer can record ground motion by recording the numerical value of the ground height at each second. This produces a list of numbers that shows the ground motion, second by second. The disadvantage of digital signals is that you do not have a record of any signals that occurred in between each sampling. One advantage is that once you have recorded the signal as a set of numbers, you can store it on a computer or other digital device. Digital recordings can also be edited easily by just changing the numbers.

Sampling Rate

The quality of digital media depends on the length of the recording intervals. The term *sampling rate* refers to how often a signal is recorded or converted to digital code. More data are captured and recorded the more times the event is sampled (**Figure 5**). For example, a digital music file with a high sampling rate may sound richer and more detailed than a file with a lower sampling rate. The downside of a higher sampling rate is that the file size is larger.

Scientists and music producers have conducted tests with people to find a sampling rate that will produce digital music files that sound realistic without having more data than humans can perceive. If the sampling rate is too high and the files are too large, then the files will waste space on music players, mobile phones, computers, or storage services.

INTERACTIVITY

Compare analog and digital signals, and learn about signal noise.

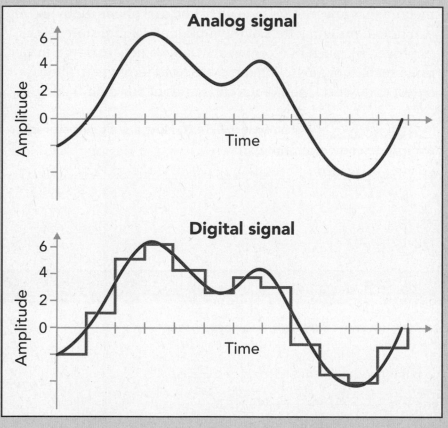

Analog signal

Digital signal

Analog-to-Digital Processing

Figure 5 When an analog signal is converted to a digital signal, what was continuous must be broken into discrete pieces. The higher the sampling rate, the closer the digital signal will come to the analog signal.

Develop Models ✏ Draw two digital versions of the original analog signal in the blank graphs: one based on sampling the analog signal 24 times, and the other based on sampling 32 times.

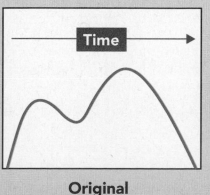

Original

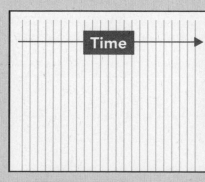

Sampled 24 times

Sampled 32 times

HANDS-ON LAB

Investigate Explore how analog signals can be converted to digital information.

Binary Code

Figure 6 The binary codes, or bytes, for the first five letters of the alphabet are shown here. Notice that there are different codes for lowercase and uppercase letters.

a = 01100001 A = 01000001
b = 01100010 B = 01000010
c = 01100011 C = 01000011
d = 01100100 D = 01000100
e = 01100101 E = 01000101

Interpret Data What would the code be for the word *Dad*?

Binary Signals

Binary Signals Recall that Morse code has just two signals—dots and dashes—that are used in different combinations to communicate letters. Computers use a similar system called binary, which consists of ones and zeros. The information that we store on computers is encoded with binary, whether it's a song, a text document, or a movie.

Each number in binary code is a bit of information. Bits are arranged into groups of eight, called bytes. The code for each letter of the alphabet has its own unique byte, as shown in **Figure 6**. The code for a word consists of bytes strung together. For example, as the author wrote this page, a computer program translated the keyboard strokes for the letters in the word *"code"* into bytes.

01100011011011110110010001100101

The basic unit of a computer's storage capacity is the byte. A megabyte is one million bytes. This means one megabyte (MB) can hold a million letters of the alphabet. Digital storage has improved so much in recent years that we now use even larger units such as gigabyte (billion bytes) and terabyte (trillion bytes) to describe the storage capacities of our digital devices.

☑ READING CHECK **Summarize Text** How are signals stored and processed on computers?

Math Toolbox
Cryptography

Cryptography is the study of codes. Use the chart in **Figure 6** to answer the following questions and "break" the codes.

1. Patterns What do you think the binary codes for the letters *f* and *F* are?

2. Draw Comparative Inferences The binary code for the number 6 is 00110110. How does this compare to the code for *f*? What can you infer about the structures of these codes?

Transmitting Signals

Modern forms of communication involve the transmission of electronic or electromagnetic signals. Many transmissions are now in digital formats. In some cases, the transmission consists of an entire file, such as a digital song file saved to your phone. In other cases, the transmission is more like a broadcast, such as a live stream.

Sound Information Analog telephones transmit signals by first converting sound waves to electronic wave pulses. Those travel along wires to another phone, which converts the wave pulses back to sound waves. Modern mobile phones convert sound waves to digital data in the form of binary code. The data are transmitted as microwaves, which are converted back to sound waves by another mobile phone. If someone records and sends a voice message from one mobile phone to another, or to a computer, the process is basically the same. Sound waves are the initial signal and the ultimate product.

INTERACTIVITY

Analyze a model of how phone calls are made with mobile devices.

Academic Vocabulary

In your science notebook, record other uses of the term *transmission* in science. In those other contexts, what's being transmitted?

Digital Audio

Figure 7 To transmit a sound signal from one place to another, the signal must be processed and converted into different forms.

Develop Models 🖊 Complete the diagram by identifying the type of signals that are being transmitted.

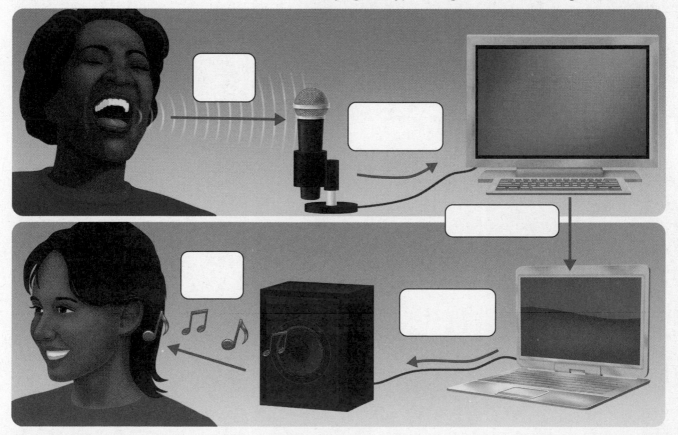

INTERACTIVITY

Model how the number of pixels affects the resolution of digital images.

Pixels and File Size

Figure 8 The three images of the flower are copies of the same file. The leftmost image has a low resolution and small file size. The middle image has higher resolution and a larger file size. The rightmost image has the highest resolution and largest file size.

Visual Information Photographs, printed documents, and other visuals can be digitized and transmitted as well. A digital visual consists of pixels, or small uniform shapes that are combined to make a larger image (**Figure 8**). The information that determines a pixel's color and brightness is coded in bytes. The more pixels that are used, the more bytes the digital image file will require. For example, a digital image that is meant to take up a few centimeters on a mobile phone screen may be far less than a megabyte, whereas an image that is meant to be shown on a high-resolution display or printed as a poster can be 50 megabytes and more. Just as audio engineers and music producers try to balance file size with detail that will be audible to human ears, visual artists and engineers must strike a balance too. They don't want their images to appear too "pixilated," but they don't want to waste device storage with too much detail either.

READING CHECK **Summarize Text** How are pixels used to capture and convey visual information with digital technology?

....

....

....

☑ LESSON 2 Check

MS-PS4-3

1. **Identify** Sound waves move from a guitar to a microphone. The microphone converts the sound waves to electronic wave pulses that are transmitted through a wire to a computer. The computer converts the wave pulses to a series of 1's and 0's. The 1's and 0's are packaged as a file and posted online for sale to the guitarist's fans. In this process, when were the signals digital?

....

....

....

....

2. **Calculate** If one letter of the alphabet is one byte, and the average word consists of five letters, how many words could be encoded in binary and stored on a 1-GB memory card?

....

....

....

....

....

3. **Make Comparative Inferences** How is the sampling rate used in recording digital music similar to the number of pixels in a digital image?

....

....

....

....

....

....

4. **Summarize Text** Compare and contrast Morse code and binary code.

....

....

....

....

....

....

....

....

....

Quest CHECK-IN

In this lesson, you learned about different types of signals and how they are used to record and transmit information.

Evaluate Why is it important to know the different types of signals that can be used to record information?

....

....

....

....

....

INTERACTIVITY

Analog and Digital Recordings

Go online to investigate and identify advantages and disadvantages of digital music.

MS-PS4-3

Super Ultra High Definition!

If your family has purchased a new television recently, you know there are many digital options. In fact, many consumers and digital media providers have sometimes struggled to keep up with the technological changes.

Video resolution is one of the most important factors in digital TV technology. Resolution refers to the number of pixels on the TV screen. The diagram shows the different resolutions currently in use. The numbers shown for each resolution refer to the dimensions of the screen image in pixels. For example, standard-definition resolution (SD) has a 640 × 480 pixel dimension. The image is made up of 480 horizontal lines. Each line contains 640 pixels, for a total of 307,200 pixels.

As resolution increases, image quality increases because there are more pixels to form the image. However, as resolution and image quality increase, file size increases too. Each pixel in the image takes up 1 byte of storage. This means that one frame of an SD image takes up 307,200 bytes, or about 0.3 megabytes (MB) of storage. A moving TV image runs at 30 frames per second, so a one-hour program would take up about 32,400 MB in storage. This is where video codecs come in. A codec is software that digitally encodes and compresses the video signal to reduce its file size without affecting image quality very much.

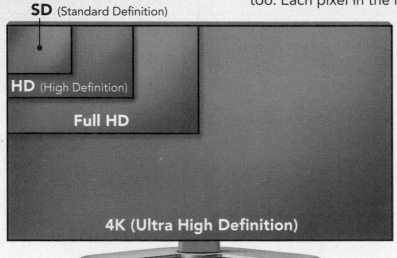

SD (Standard Definition)

HD (High Definition)

Full HD

4K (Ultra High Definition)

A Streaming Society

Today, many people download or stream TV shows and movies to their televisions and smart devices. Because the higher-quality signals are larger in file size, fast Internet speeds are required to move all the data. Internet speed is generally measured in megabits per second (Mbps). The amount of data that can be transferred at three different speeds is shown here.

Mbps speed	MB transferred per second
1	0.125
50	6.25
100	12.5

Use the text and data to answer the following questions.

1. **Use Models** A 4K image contains 8,294,400 pixels. What is the corresponding file size?

2. **Calculate** Suppose you're downloading a movie that is 3.2 GB. Your Internet speed is 50 Mbps. About how long will it take to download the file? Show your work.

3. **Patterns** Some video engineers are already touting 8K resolution, the next advance in video technology. The image quality of an 8K signal is equal to taking four 4K TVs and arranging them in a 2 × 2 array. What are the dimensions of an 8K image? Explain.

4. **Analyze Properties** Television programs used to be transmitted using analog signals. As more people began to buy HD televisions and watch HD programming, TV broadcasters and cable providers switched to digital signals. Why do you think this switch occurred? What advantage does a digital signal have over an analog signal when transmitting HD video?

5. **Construct Explanations** Most televisions sold now are 4K Ultra HD capable. However, most streaming services and digital TV providers offer little 4K programming. Why do think this is the case?

LESSON

3 Communication and Technology

Guiding Questions

- What technologies are used for communication?
- What are the advantages of using digital signals for communications technology?

Connections

Literacy Cite Textual Evidence

Math Analyze Relationships

MS-PS4-3

HANDS-ON LAB

uInvestigate Observe the structure of a vinyl record and predict how it functions.

Vocabulary

information technology
software
noise
bandwidth

Academic Vocabulary

hardware

Connect It!

✏ **Circle a symbol on the clay tablet that appears more than once.**

Compare and Contrast How is the ancient clay tablet similar to a digital tablet of today? How is it different?

....

....

....

....

The Information Age

The invention of writing was one of the first examples of information technology. Using a sharpened stick or a finger and some kind of medium such as clay (**Figure 1**) or a stone wall, people were able to record ideas, observations, and other information.

Fast forward to today. Information technology is everywhere, and there many forms and modes of writing. For example, one person typed the text on this page into a computer. The file was then sent via the internet to reviewers and editors. Edited text was then combined with the photograph in a different computer application. Finally, a file was sent to a printer, and a series of pages were put together as a book. What would have taken hours to inscribe in clay or rock can now be recorded and shared much faster, thanks to information technology. Modern Information technology consists of computer and telecommunications hardware and software that store, transmit, receive, and manipulate information. Software refers to programs that encode, decode, and interpret information, including browsers, apps, games, and operating systems. The invention of electronic computers around 1940 helped usher in the information age.

INTERACTIVITY

Discuss the encoding and decoding of information with classmates.

Academic Vocabulary

Hardware is an older term. What do you think "hard" refers to in the information technology usage of *hardware*?

....

....

....

Sumerian Tablet

Figure 1 This clay tablet was used to record information 6,500 years ago in Sumer, part of Mesopotamia.

Server Farm

Figure 2 This facility has thousands of computers that store and share the data of millions of people.

Ask Questions Why do think this facility is called a server farm?

....

....

....

....

Literacy Connection

Cite Textual Evidence
Underline text that supports the idea that we are in a period of exponential data growth.

Information Technologies Every day, hundreds of millions of e-mails, and billions of text messages are sent. Files are also exchanged online through "clouds" that are accessible from thousands of networks. Every year, trillions of gigabytes of information are produced on Earth, ranging from high-definition movies to printable text documents to brief messages about what to buy at the supermarket.

The software and hardware that power modern information technology (IT) depend on each other. IT hardware is the modern version of clay or stone. It serves as the physical medium where information is stored and altered. Processor chips, batteries, disks, wiring, and other components compose the physical place where software operates. In some cases, the hardware you depend on is "local," such as the processor, display, built-in memory, and other components of your mobile device or computer. Other hardware that you probably use is housed elsewhere, such as the cell phone tower that may be in or near your town, and the "farms" of servers that major telecommunications and computer companies use to store some of your information (**Figure 2**). By accessing data held on a server that is somewhere else, you can watch, listen to, read, or otherwise experience media without actually storing the data locally. We are now in a period of exponential growth of digital information production.

READING CHECK **Summarize Text** What are some examples of hardware used in information technology?

....

....

....

Communications Systems

Before the industrial and information ages, long-distance communication methods included smoke signals and handwritten messages carried by pigeons. Today, we depend on three types of transmissions: electronic signals carried by wires, electromagnetic transmissions through the atmosphere, and electromagnetic transmissions through fiber-optic cables.

  VIDEO

Learn about the career of a network administrator.

Math Toolbox

Digital Data Explosion

With ever-growing numbers of people accessing the Internet, greater and greater amounts of information and data are being produced. The graph shows data production and expected projections for the future.

1. **Interpret Data** Compare the rate of growth from 2011 to 2013 with the rate of growth from 2015 to 2017.

....

....

....

....

....

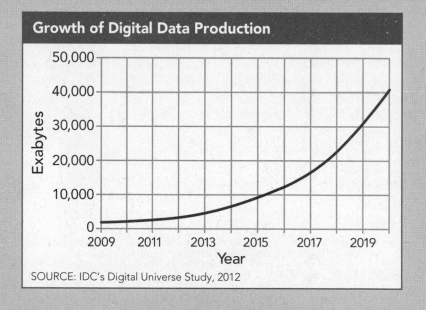

Growth of Digital Data Production

SOURCE: IDC's Digital Universe Study, 2012

2. **Analyze Relationships** What do you think accounts for the exponential growth of data in recent years?

....

....

....

....

3. **Patterns** If the trend continues, how much data will be produced in 2030?

....

....

....

....

....

Roger That!

Figure 3 Communications technologies all have one thing in common—they must move vast amounts of data in our digital world.

Connect to Technology For each type of communications technology, identify a benefit and a drawback of using analog signals and digital signals.

For many years, radio and television broadcasts were transmitted using radio waves. Analog televisions and radios depended on tall towers to broadcast signals over the air. In recent years, television has switched over to digital signal transmissions. Televisions can now handle high definition media.

Making a telephone call used to involve a large device mounted on a wall or in a booth, which was wired to a switchboard operator in another location, who would connect your call to a specific person by connecting two circuits. There was no "voicemail" system to record a message. The signal could be poor, making it difficult to hear each other. Nowadays, many people carry phones in their pockets that can connect to other people around the world.

Benefit

....

....

Drawback

....

....

Benefit

....

....

Drawback

....

....

Telecommunications satellites that orbit Earth can relay signals that cannot be transmitted by wires or towers. Some satellites are used to broadcast television stations and other media, and others are used by government agencies and the military.

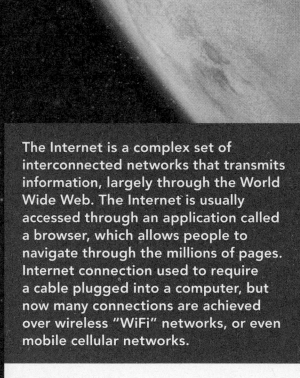

Benefit

....

....

Drawback

....

....

Fiber optic technology is based on glass or plastic cables that transmit light at speeds around 200,000 kilometers per second. Fiber-optic cables can carry about a thousand times more information per second than standard copper cable.

Benefit

....

....

Drawback

....

....

The Internet is a complex set of interconnected networks that transmits information, largely through the World Wide Web. The Internet is usually accessed through an application called a browser, which allows people to navigate through the millions of pages. Internet connection used to require a cable plugged into a computer, but now many connections are achieved over wireless "WiFi" networks, or even mobile cellular networks.

Benefit

....

....

Drawback

....

....

Advantages of Digital Signals

Although they are not continuous signals, digital signals are more reliable and efficient overall than analog signals, for several reasons.

Compatibility with Computers
Computers process digital signals, and computers are everywhere—on laps and desktops, tucked in pockets, in car dashboards, and even on refrigerator doors. It's easier for computers and digital devices to do what we want them to do without having to convert analog signals first. Using digitals signals is more efficient.

Noise
When an analog signal is transmitted, it can incorporate noise—random signals from the environment. This noise can then stay with the signal and alter the output. Static is an example of noise. Because digital signals consist of 0's and 1's, it is more difficult for noise to alter the signal, because binary code is essentially a choice between on and off. Unless noise causes a one to become a zero or vice versa, noise shouldn't affect how the digital signal is received or read.

Model It!

Noise? No Problem!
The first graph shows an analog signal accompanied by noise during transmission. The second graph shows a digital signal also accompanied by noise during transmission.

Develop Models ✏
Complete the models by drawing the received analog and digital signals to show how noise affects each one.

Original signal with noise

Analog signal

Noise

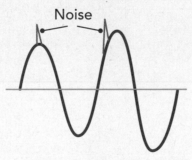

Digital signal

Noise

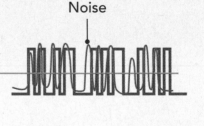

Received signal

Distortion caused by noise   Restored digital signal

Security Although digital signals are encrypted—hidden by binary coding—both analog and digital signals are vulnerable to security breaches. It's relatively easy for someone to tap into an analog phone line and listen to or record the conversation, because the signal is not encrypted. It's more difficult to access digital phone signals or communications, but hacking—stealing of digital information by breaking the codes—is on the rise. Tech experts are continually working to improve digital security.

INTERACTIVITY

Research the advantages and disadvantages of analog and digital signals.

Bandwidth As illustrated in **Figure 4**, the amount of information that can be transmitted and measured in bits per second is called **bandwidth**. Digital signals carry less information than comparable analog signals, so digital information technology solutions typically have greater bandwidth than analog solutions. For example, a cable that provides a home with television and Internet service can provide those services faster, and allow more data to be downloaded and uploaded, if it carries digital signals. Compression can help with bandwidth as well. For example, if a 1-gigabyte file can be compressed to a smaller file size for transmission and then uncompressed by a computer, the file should download faster.

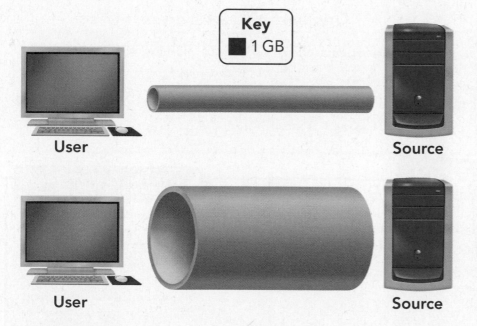

Bandwidth

Figure 4 Narrow bandwidth means slower data transmission, which likely means slower download times.

Develop Models ✎ Using the information in the key, model the transmission of 5 GB of data from each source to each user. Your model should demonstrate why narrower bandwidth results in slower download times.

☑ READING CHECK **Cite Textual Evidence** Why are there so many different types of communications technology?

....

....

☑ LESSON 3 Check

1. Identify List five different technologies or types of hardware that are used today in communications.

....

....

....

....

....

2. Cause and Effect Describe how increasing bandwidth and improving compression software can result in a higher quality of hardware and media of higher resolution.

....

....

....

....

....

....

....

....

....

3. Summarize What role does software play in information technology?

....

....

....

4. Construct Explanations Explain why digital signals are somewhat harder to hack or spy on than analog signals.

....

....

....

....

....

....

....

....

....

....

....

....

Quest CHECK-IN

In this lesson, you learned about information technology and the advantages of using digital signals for communication.

Evaluate How do hardware and infrastructure affect how we use signals?

....

....

....

....

....

👆 INTERACTIVITY

Evaluate Recording Technologies

Go online to research scientific and technical information about analog and digital recording technologies. Then, present your findings in a poster.

Beam Me Up!

It may be hard to believe, but using your phone to make a video call to a friend or family member on the other side of the planet was the stuff of science fiction until about a decade ago. Although the idea for video calls can be traced back to the late 1800s, it required a great deal of scientific advancement and technological progress to become a reality.

In the 1930s, following the development of television, German scientists developed a closed-circuit TV system that allowed people to talk to each other in different cities. Despite plans to expand, the system was shut down in 1940 following the outbreak of World War II.

At the 1964 World's Fair in New York, an American telecommunications company unveiled a picture phone to the world. The system used a regular telephone line with a separate video screen. Since it was very expensive, it did not catch on with the public.

In the 1980s and 1990s, technological advancements, spurred on by the growing popularity of personal computers, led to the development of videoconferencing technology. As electronic devices shrank, it was only a matter of time before the technology made it to the palms of our hands.

MY DISCOVERY

Type "video telephony" into an online search engine to learn more about the history of this technology.

☑TOPIC 2 Review and Assess

1 Electric Circuits

MS-PS4-3

1. Which of the following is *not* a basic part of an electric circuit?
   A. conducting wires
   B. a transformer
   C. a source of electrical energy
   D. a device that runs on electrical energy

2. In a typical battery,
   A. the negative end has more electrical potential energy than the positive end.
   B. the negative end has the same amount of electrical potential energy as the positive end.
   C. the positive end has more electrical potential energy than the negative end.
   D. voltage determines which end of the battery has more electrical potential energy.

3. The measure of how hard it is for current to flow through an object is called ....

4. Develop Models ✏ Draw a diagram of a circuit that consists of two lights. The circuit must allow for one light to remain lit if the other light bulb goes out.

2 Signals

MS-PS4-3

5. Digital signals rely on a coding system known as
   A. megabytes.   B. transmission.
   C. wave pulse.   D. binary.

6. Which of the following comparisons between analog and digital signals is correct?
   A. Analog signals are electronic signals, while digital signals are electromagnetic signals.
   B. Analog signals are continuous signals, while digital signals are discrete signals.
   C. Analog signals can be stored on computers, while digital signals cannot.
   D. Analog signals store information as numbers, while digital signals do not.

7. Evaluate Claims A friend says that digital signals are more exact representations than analog signals. Do you agree? Explain.

....
....
....
....
....

8. Communicate Using a real-world example, identify one advantage of a digital signal over an analog signal.

....
....
....
....
....
....
....
....

3 Communication and Technology

MS-PS4-3

9. Which of the following is *not* an advantage of sending an email over sending a letter through the postal service?
   A. The email is encrypted, making it harder for someone to intercept and read.
   B. The email is easier to store and retrieve, making it less likely to get lost.
   C. The email is more likely to get destroyed.
   D. The email will arrive much faster than the mailed letter.

10. Which of the following statements about signal noise is true?
    A. It affects analog and digital signals in similar ways.
    B. It affects digital signals more than analog signals.
    C. It affects analog signals more than digital signals.
    D. It has little effect on either analog or digital signals.

11. The amount of information that can be transmitted as digital signals over some amount of time is known as
    A. bandwidth.   B. hardware.
    C. resolution.   D. noise.

12. Information technology consists of .... and ....that store, manipulate, and transmit information.

13. **Analyze Systems** Why is fiber optic technology an improvement over standard copper cable?

    ....

    ....

    ....

14. **Connect to Nature of Science** Choose an example of a digital technology and describe how it has helped to advance science and scientific investigations.

    ....

    ....

    ....

    ....

    ....

    ....

    ....

    ....

15. **Construct Explanations** Explain why digital signals are a more reliable way to conduct a telephone conversation.

    ....

    ....

    ....

    ....

    ....

    ....

    ....

    ....

MS-PS4-3

Evidence-Based Assessment

A friend of yours lives in a nearby town. The town needs to purchase new two-way radios for its emergency first responders. Town board members are considering replacing the two-way analog radios with digital radios.

However, the digital radios are more expensive. Board members want to know whether the increased costs will bring any benefits before they will vote to approve the measure. Many residents are opposed to spending additional money on new technology.

You and your friend research the issue and find the graph shown here, which compares the range and quality of analog radio signals with digital radio signals.

Range and Quality of Analog and Digital Radios

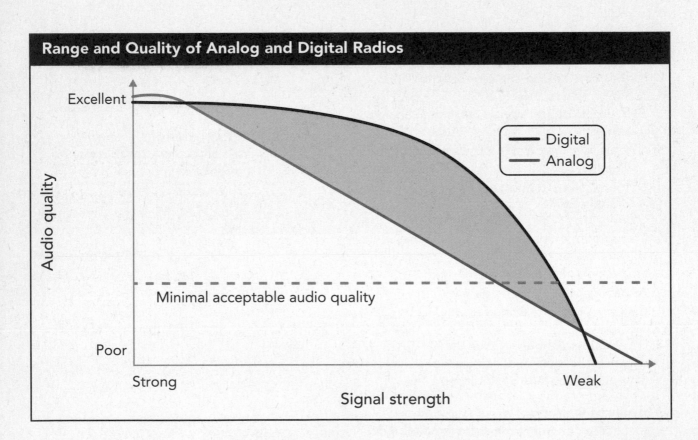

1. **Interpret Data** What does the shaded part of the graph represent?
   A. area in which the audio quality of both radios is not affected by signal strength
   B. area of the digital radio's improved performance over the analog radio
   C. area in which there is no difference in quality between the analog and digital radios
   D. area of the analog radio's improved performance over the digital radio

2. **Characterize Data** Which of the following statements about the data in the graph are correct? Select all that apply.
   ☐ The audio quality of the analog radio is slightly better with a very strong signal.
   ☐ The digital radio has improved audio quality with the very weakest signals.
   ☐ Both the analog and digital radio have almost the same quality with moderate signal strengths.
   ☐ The audio quality of the analog radios drops more sharply as signal strength weakens.

3. **Use Graphs** How are signal strength and audio quality related for both analog and digital signals?

   ....
   ....
   ....
   ....
   ....

4. **Cite Evidence** Use evidence from the graph to explain why the digital radio signals are more reliable than the analog radio signals.

   ....
   ....
   ....
   ....
   ....

5. **Construct Arguments** What can your friend tell the town board members and residents to persuade them to purchase the digital radios?

   ....
   ....
   ....
   ....
   ....
   ....
   ....
   ....

Quest FINDINGS

Complete the Quest!

Phenomenon Determine the best way to present your claim in a multimedia presentation.

Connect to Society Are there situations in which recording with an analog signal would be more reliable than a digital signal? Explain.

....
....
....

INTERACTIVITY

Reflect on Your Recording Method

Over and Out

How can you demonstrate that **digital** signals are a more efficient way to send **information**?

Background

The Center for Information Technology Education will soon open its doors to the public. The center houses a library for students and researchers, as well as a large multimedia theater and exhibit areas. The center has devoted space for hands-on exhibits where visitors can explore communication technology and its history. The center wants you to develop an interactive exhibit that compares and contrasts analog and digital signals. The exhibit's models will allow visitors to send a coded signal designed for each transmission method.

In this investigation, you will design models that help visitors recognize that digital signals are a more reliable way than analog signals to transmit data and information.

Materials

(per group)

- spring coil
- small light bulb and socket
- battery (9-volt or type C)
- electrical wire, 10 strips
- electrical switch

Safety

Be sure to follow all safety guidelines provided by your teacher. The Safety Appendix of your textbook provides more details about the safety icons.

1885

1920

1985

2015

In just over 125 years, telephone technology has evolved from large boxes with a lot of wires to small, wireless powerhouses.

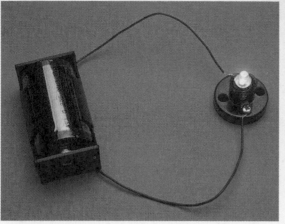 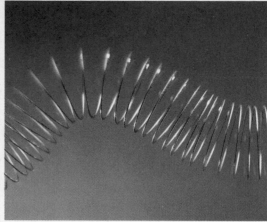

Design Your Exhibit Model

1. Plan the models you will use in the exhibit. Think about how you can use the available materials to represent two different communication systems: one that models how analog signals send information using continuous wave pulses and one that models how digital signals send information using discrete wave pulses. Consider the following questions as you plan and design your model:

   • Is the spring coil or an electric circuit a better choice to represent the continuous nature of analog signals?

   • Which of these materials is more appropriate to model the discrete nature of digital signals?

2. Develop a code that can be used for the analog system and another one that can be used for the digital system. The data you will transmit is a word made up of four letters: E, T, A, and S. You will need to create a code for each letter. Think about the following questions as you develop the codes:

   • How can you use continuous wave pulses of different amplitudes to represent each letter for the analog system?

   • How can you use discrete wave pulses to represent each letter for the digital system?

3. Sketch your models in the space provided and label the materials you will use. Include descriptions of how the models will operate. Then, complete the table with the codes you developed.

4. After getting your teacher's approval, carry out your investigation. One team member is the transmitter and the other member is the receiver. The transmitter should choose a word, refer to the code, and then transmit the word using the analog system. Repeat the process using a different word for the digital system. You may want to consider using commands to indicate the start and end of transmissions, such as "start transmission" and "end transmission." Run the trial again using the same procedure for each system.

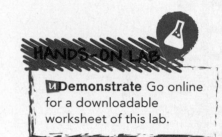

HANDS-ON LAB

Demonstrate Go online for a downloadable worksheet of this lab.

uDemonstrate Lab

Model Sketches

Data Table and Observations

Letter	Analog Code	Digital Code
E		
T		
A		
S		

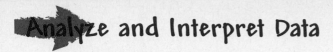

Analyze and Interpret Data

1. **Use Models** Describe the results of your investigation and your observations about using each system to transmit information. Which system did you find easier to use? Which system was more accurate? Explain.

....

....

....

....

2. **Explain Phenomena** Think about the issue of signal noise. How could you incorporate this concept into your models? What effect do you think signal noise would have on the analog system? What effect might it have on the digital system?

....

....

....

....

3. **Communicate** How do your models for the exhibit demonstrate that digital signals are a more reliable way to encode and transmit information than analog signals? Explain.

....

....

....

....

4. **Identify Limitations** What are some of the challenges you faced as you designed your models and codes? What are some of the drawbacks or limitations of your models?

....

....

....

....

....

SEP.1, SEP.8

The Meaning of Science

Science Skills

Science is a way of learning about the natural world. It involves asking questions, making predictions, and collecting information to see if the answer is right or wrong.

The table lists some of the skills that scientists use. You use some of these skills every day. For example, you may observe and evaluate your lunch options before choosing what to eat.

Reflect Think about a time you misplaced something and could not find it. Write a sentence defining the problem. What science skills could you use to solve the problem? Explain how you would use at least three of the skills in the table.

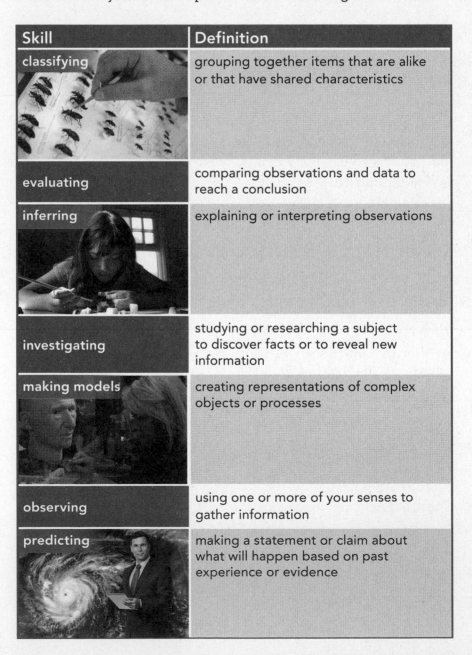

Skill	Definition
classifying	grouping together items that are alike or that have shared characteristics
evaluating	comparing observations and data to reach a conclusion
inferring	explaining or interpreting observations
investigating	studying or researching a subject to discover facts or to reveal new information
making models	creating representations of complex objects or processes
observing	using one or more of your senses to gather information
predicting	making a statement or claim about what will happen based on past experience or evidence

Scientific Attitudes

Curiosity often drives scientists to learn about the world around them. Creativity is useful for coming up with inventive ways to solve problems. Such qualities and attitudes, and the ability to keep an open mind, are essential for scientists.

When sharing results or findings, honesty and ethics are also essential. Ethics refers to rules for knowing right from wrong.

Being skeptical is also important. This means having doubts about things based on past experiences and evidence. Skepticism helps to prevent accepting data and results that may not be true.

Scientists must also avoid bias—likes or dislikes of people, ideas, or things. They must avoid experimental bias, which is a mistake that may make an experiment's preferred outcome more likely.

Scientific Reasoning

Scientific reasoning depends on being logical and objective. When you are objective, you use evidence and apply logic to draw conclusions. Being subjective means basing conclusions on personal feelings, biases, or opinions. Subjective reasoning can interfere with science and skew results. Objective reasoning helps scientists use observations to reach conclusions about the natural world.

Scientists use two types of objective reasoning: deductive and inductive. Deductive reasoning involves starting with a general idea or theory and applying it to a situation. For example, the theory of plate tectonics indicates that earthquakes happen mostly where tectonic plates meet. You could then draw the conclusion, or deduce, that California has many earthquakes because tectonic plates meet there.

In inductive reasoning, you make a generalization from a specific observation. When scientists collect data in an experiment and draw a conclusion based on that data, they use inductive reasoning. For example, if fertilizer causes one set of plants to grow faster than another, you might infer that the fertilizer promotes plant growth.

Make Meaning
Think about a bias the marine biologist in the photo could show that results in paying more or less attention to one kind of organism over others. Make a prediction about how that bias could affect the biologist's survey of the coral reef.

Write About It
Suppose it is raining when you go to sleep one night. When you wake up the next morning, you observe frozen puddles on the ground and icicles on tree branches. Use scientific reasoning to draw a conclusion about the air temperature outside. Support your conclusion using deductive or inductive reasoning.

SEP.1, SEP.2, SEP.3, SEP.4, CCC.4

Science Processes

Scientific Inquiry

Scientists contribute to scientific knowledge by conducting investigations and drawing conclusions. The process often begins with an observation that leads to a question, which is then followed by the development of a hypothesis. This is known as scientific inquiry.

One of the first steps in scientific inquiry is asking questions. However, it's important to make a question specific with a narrow focus so the investigation will not be too broad. A biologist may want to know all there is to know about wolves, for example. But a good, focused question for a specific inquiry might be "How many offspring does the average female wolf produce in her lifetime?"

A hypothesis is a possible answer to a scientific question. A hypothesis must be testable. For something to be testable, researchers must be able to carry out an investigation and gather evidence that will either support or disprove the hypothesis.

Scientific Models

Models are tools that scientists use to study phenomena indirectly. A model is any representation of an object or process. Illustrations, dioramas, globes, diagrams, computer programs, and mathematical equations are all examples of scientific models. For example, a diagram of Earth's crust and mantle can help you to picture layers deep below the surface and understand events such as volcanic eruptions.

Models also allow scientists to represent objects that are either very large, such as our solar system, or very small, such as a molecule of DNA. Models can also represent processes that occur over a long period of time, such as the changes that have occurred throughout Earth's history.

Models are helpful, but they have limitations. Physical models are not made of the same materials as the objects they represent. Most models of complex objects or processes show only major parts, stages, or relationships. Many details are left out. Therefore, you may not be able to learn as much from models as you would through direct observation.

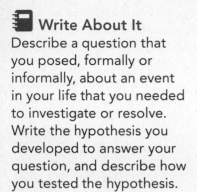

Write About It Describe a question that you posed, formally or informally, about an event in your life that you needed to investigate or resolve. Write the hypothesis you developed to answer your question, and describe how you tested the hypothesis.

Reflect Identify the benefits and limitations of using a plastic model of DNA, as shown here.

Science Experiments

An experiment or investigation must be well planned to produce valid results. In planning an experiment, you must identify the independent and dependent variables. You must also do as much as possible to remove the effects of other variables. A controlled experiment is one in which you test only one variable at a time.

For example, suppose you plan a controlled experiment to learn how the type of material affects the speed at which sound waves travel through it. The only variable that should change is the type of material. This way, if the speed of sound changes, you know that it is a result of a change in the material, not another variable such as the thickness of the material or the type of sound used.

You should also remove bias from any investigation. You may inadvertently introduce bias by selecting subjects you like and avoiding those you don't like. Scientists often conduct investigations by taking random samples to avoid ending up with biased results.

Once you plan your investigation and begin to collect data, it's important to record and organize the data. You may wish to use a graph to display and help you to interpret the data.

Communicating is the sharing of ideas and results with others through writing and speaking. Communicating data and conclusions is a central part of science.

Scientists share knowledge, including new findings, theories, and techniques for collecting data. Conferences, journals, and websites help scientists to communicate with each other. Popular media, including newspapers, magazines, and social media sites, help scientists to share their knowledge with nonscientists. However, before the results of investigations are shared and published, other scientists should review the experiment for possible sources of error, such as bias and unsupported conclusions.

Write About It
List four ways you could communicate the results of a scientific study about the health of sea turtles in the Pacific Ocean.

SEP.1, SEP.6, SEP.7, SEP.8

Scientific Knowledge

Scientific Explanations

Suppose you learn that adult flamingos are pink because of the food they eat. This statement is a scientific explanation— it describes how something in nature works or explains why it happens. Scientists from different fields use methods such as researching information, designing experiments, and making models to form scientific explanations. Scientific explanations often result from many years of work and multiple investigations conducted by many scientists.

Scientific Theories and Laws

A scientific law is a statement that describes what you can expect to occur every time under a particular set of conditions. A scientific law describes an observed pattern in nature, but it does not attempt to explain it. For example, the law of superposition describes what you can expect to find in terms of the ages of layers of rock. Geologists use this observed pattern to determine the relative ages of sedimentary rock layers. But the law does not explain why the pattern occurs.

By contrast, a scientific theory is a well-tested explanation for a wide range of observations or experimental results. It provides details and describes causes of observed patterns. Something is elevated to a theory only when there is a large body of evidence that supports it. However, a scientific theory can be changed or overturned when new evidence is found.

Write About It
Choose two fields of science that interest you. Describe a method used to develop scientific explanations in each field.

Compare and Contrast Complete the table to compare and contrast a scientific theory and a scientific law.

	Scientific Theory	Scientific Law
Definition		
Does it attempt to explain a pattern observed in nature?		

Analyzing Scientific Explanations

To analyze scientific explanations that you hear on the news or read in a book such as this one, you need scientific literacy. Scientific literacy means understanding scientific terms and principles well enough to ask questions, evaluate information, and make decisions. Scientific reasoning gives you a process to apply. This includes looking for bias and errors in the research, evaluating data, and identifying faulty reasoning. For example, by evaluating how a survey was conducted, you may find a serious flaw in the researchers' methods.

Evidence and Opinions

The basis for scientific explanations is empirical evidence. Empirical evidence includes the data and observations that have been collected through scientific processes. Satellite images, photos, and maps of mountains and volcanoes are all examples of empirical evidence that support a scientific explanation about Earth's tectonic plates. Scientists look for patterns when they analyze this evidence. For example, they might see a pattern that mountains and volcanoes often occur near tectonic plate boundaries.

To evaluate scientific information, you must first distinguish between evidence and opinion. In science, evidence includes objective observations and conclusions that have been repeated. Evidence may or may not support a scientific claim. An opinion is a subjective idea that is formed from evidence, but it cannot be confirmed by evidence.

Write About It

Suppose the conservation committee of a town wants to gauge residents' opinions about a proposal to stock the local ponds with fish every spring. The committee pays for a survey to appear on a web site that is popular with people who like to fish. The results of the survey show 78 people in favor of the proposal and two against it. Do you think the survey's results are valid? Explain.

Make Meaning

Explain what empirical evidence the photograph reveals.

SEP.3, SEP.4

Tools of Science

Measurement

Making measurements using standard units is important in all fields of science. This allows scientists to repeat and reproduce other experiments, as well as to understand the precise meaning of the results of others. Scientists use a measurement system called the International System of Units, or SI.

For each type of measurement, there is a series of units that are greater or less than each other. The unit a scientist uses depends on what is being measured. For example, a geophysicist tracking the movements of tectonic plates may use centimeters, as plates tend to move small amounts each year. Meanwhile, a marine biologist might measure the movement of migrating bluefin tuna on the scale of kilometers.

Units for length, mass, volume, and density are based on powers of ten—a meter is equal to 100 centimeters or 1000 millimeters. Units of time do not follow that pattern. There are 60 seconds in a minute, 60 minutes in an hour, and 24 hours in a day. These units are based on patterns that humans perceived in nature. Units of temperature are based on scales that are set according to observations of nature. For example, 0°C is the temperature at which pure water freezes, and 100°C is the temperature at which it boils.

Write About It
Suppose you are planning an investigation in which you must measure the dimensions of several small mineral samples that fit in your hand. Which metric unit or units will you most likely use? Explain your answer.

Measurement	Metric units
Length or distance	meter (m), kilometer (km), centimeter (cm), millimeter (mm) 1 km = 1,000 m 1 cm = 10 mm 1 m = 100 cm
Mass	kilogram (kg), gram (g), milligram (mg) 1 kg = 1,000 g 1 g = 1,000 mg
Volume	cubic meter (m^3), cubic centimeter (cm^3) 1 m^3 = 1,000,000 cm^3
Density	kilogram per cubic meter (kg/m^3), gram per cubic centimeter (g/cm^3) 1,000 kg/m^3 = 1 g/cm^3
Temperature	degrees Celsius (°C), kelvin (K) 1°C = 273 K
Time	hour (h), minute (m), second (s)

Math Skills

Using numbers to collect and interpret data involves math skills that are essential in science. For example, you use math skills when you estimate the number of birds in an entire forest after counting the actual number of birds in ten trees.

Scientists evaluate measurements and estimates for their precision and accuracy. In science, an accurate measurement is very close to the actual value. Precise measurements are very close, or nearly equal, to each other. Reliable measurements are both accurate and precise. An imprecise value may be a sign of an error in data collection. This kind of anomalous data may be excluded to avoid skewing the data and harming the investigation.

Other math skills include performing specific calculations, such as finding the mean, or average, value in a data set. The mean can be calculated by adding up all of the values in the data set and then dividing that sum by the number of values.

Hour	Number of Ducks Observed at a Pond
1	12
2	10
3	2
4	14
5	13
6	10
7	11

Calculate The data table shows how many ducks were seen at a pond every hour over the course of seven hours. Is there a data point that seems anomalous? If so, cross out that data point. Then, calculate the mean number of ducks on the pond. Round the mean to the nearest whole number.

Graphs

Graphs help scientists to interpret data by helping them to find trends or patterns in the data. A line graph displays data that show how one variable (the dependent or outcome variable) changes in response to another (the independent or test variable). The slope and shape of a graph line can reveal patterns and help scientists to make predictions. For example, line graphs can help you to spot patterns of change over time.

Scientists use bar graphs to compare data across categories or subjects that may not affect each other. The heights of the bars make it easy to compare those quantities. A circle graph, also known as a pie chart, shows the proportions of different parts of a whole.

Write About It
You and a friend record the distance you travel every 15 minutes on a one-hour bike trip. Your friend wants to display the data as a circle graph. Explain whether or not this is the best type of graph to display your data. If not, suggest another graph to use.

SEP.1, SEP.2, SEP.3, SEP.6

The Engineering and Design Process

Engineers are builders and problem solvers. Chemical engineers experiment with new fuels made from algae. Civil engineers design roadways and bridges. Bioengineers develop medical devices and prosthetics. The common trait among engineers is an ability to identify problems and design solutions to solve them. Engineers use a creative process that relies on scientific methods to help guide them from a concept or idea all the way to the final product.

Define the Problem

To identify or define a problem, different questions need to be asked: *What are the effects of the problem? What are the likely causes? What other factors could be involved?* Sometimes the obvious, immediate cause of a problem may be the result of another problem that may not be immediately apparent. For example, climate change results in different weather patterns, which in turn can affect organisms that live in certain habitats. So engineers must be aware of all the possible effects of potential solutions. Engineers must also take into account how well different solutions deal with the different causes of the problem.

Reflect Write about a problem that you encountered in your life that had both immediate, obvious causes as well as less-obvious and less-immediate ones.

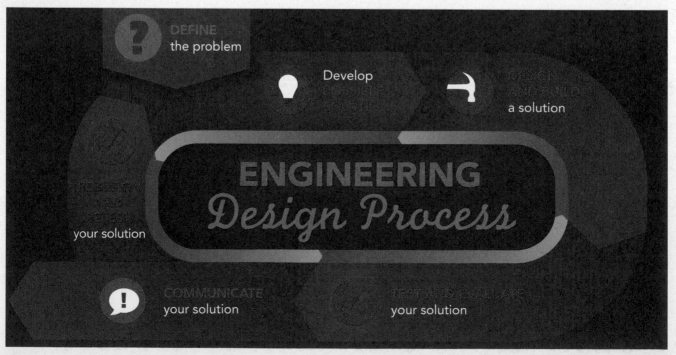

As engineers consider problems and design solutions, they must identify and categorize the criteria and constraints of the project.

Criteria are the factors that must be met or accomplished by the solution. For example, a gardener who wants to protect outdoor plants from deer and rabbits may say that the criteria for the solution are "plants are no longer eaten" and "plant growth is not inhibited in any way." The gardener then knows the plants cannot simply be sealed off from the environment, because the plants will not receive sunlight and water.

The same gardener will likely have constraints on his solution, such as budget for materials and time that is available for working on the project. By setting constraints, a solution can be designed that will be successful without introducing a new set of problems. No one wants to spend $500 on materials to protect $100 worth of tomatoes and cucumbers.

Develop Possible Solutions

After the problem has been identified, and the criteria and constraints identified, an engineer will consider possible solutions. This often involves working in teams with other engineers and designers to brainstorm ideas and research materials that can be used in the design.

It's important for engineers to think creatively and explore all potential solutions. If you wanted to design a bicycle that was safer and easier to ride than a traditional bicycle, then you would want more than just one or two solutions. Having multiple ideas to choose from increases the likelihood that you will develop a solution that meets the criteria and constraints. In addition, different ideas that result from brainstorming can often lead to new and better solutions to an existing problem.

Make Meaning
Using the example of a garden that is vulnerable to wild animals such as deer, make a list of likely constraints on an engineering solution to the problem you identified before. Determine if there are common traits among the constraints, and identify categories for them.

Design a Solution

Engineers then develop the idea that they feel best solves the problem. Once a solution has been chosen, engineers and designers get to work building a model or prototype of the solution. A model may involve sketching on paper or using computer software to construct a model of the solution. A prototype is a working model of the solution.

Building a model or prototype helps an engineer determine whether a solution meets the criteria and stays within the constraints. During this stage of the process, engineers must often deal with new problems and make any necessary adjustments to the model or prototype.

Test and Evaluate a Solution

Make Meaning Think about an aluminum beverage can. What would happen if the price or availability of aluminum changed so much that cans needed to be made of a new material? What would the criteria and constraints be on the development of a new can?

Whether testing a model or a prototype, engineers use scientific processes to evaluate their solutions. Multiple experiments, tests, or trials are conducted, data are evaluated, and results and analyses are communicated. New criteria or constraints may emerge as a result of testing. In most cases, a solution will require some refinement or revision, even if it has been through successful testing. Refining a solution is necessary if there are new constraints, such as less money or available materials. Additional testing may be done to ensure that a solution satisfies local, state, or federal laws or standards.

A naval architect sets up a model to test how the the hull's design responds to waves.

Communicate the Solution

Engineers need to communicate the final design to the people who will manufacture the product. This may include sketches, detailed drawings, computer simulations, and written text. Engineers often provide evidence that was collected during the testing stage. This evidence may include graphs and data tables that support the decisions made for the final design.

If there is feedback about the solution, then the engineers and designers must further refine the solution. This might involve making minor adjustments to the design, or it might mean bigger modifications to the design based on new criteria or constraints. Any changes in the design will require additional testing to make sure that the changes work as intended.

Redesign and Retest the Solution

At different steps in the engineering and design process, a solution usually must be revised and retested. Many designs fail to work perfectly, even after models and prototypes are built, tested, and evaluated. Engineers must be ready to analyze new results and deal with any new problems that arise. Troubleshooting, or fixing design problems, allows engineers to adjust the design to improve on how well the solution meets the need.

Communicate Suppose you are an engineer at an aerospace company. Your team is designing a rover to be used on a future NASA space mission. A family member doesn't understand why so much your team's time is taken up with testing and retesting the rover design. What are three things you would tell your relative to explain why testing and retesting are so important to the engineering and design process?

Safety Symbols

These symbols warn of possible dangers in the laboratory and remind you to work carefully.

 Safety Goggles Wear safety goggles to protect your eyes in any activity involving chemicals, flames or heating, or glassware.

 Lab Apron Wear a laboratory apron to protect your skin and clothing from damage.

 Breakage Handle breakable materials, such as glassware, with care. Do not touch broken glassware.

 Heat-Resistant Gloves Use an oven mitt or other hand protection when handling hot materials, such as hot plates or hot glassware.

 Plastic Gloves Wear disposable plastic gloves when working with harmful chemicals and organisms. Keep your hands away from your face, and dispose of the gloves according to your teacher's instructions.

 Heating Use a clamp or tongs to pick up hot glassware. Do not touch hot objects with your bare hands.

 Flames Before you work with flames, tie back loose hair and clothing. Follow your teacher's instructions about lighting and extinguishing flames.

 No Flames When using flammable materials, make sure there are no flames, sparks, or other exposed heat sources present.

 Corrosive Chemical Avoid getting acid or other corrosive chemicals on your skin or clothing or in your eyes. Do not inhale the vapors. Wash your hands after the activity.

 Poison Do not let any poisonous chemical come into contact with your skin, and do not inhale its vapors. Wash your hands when you are finished with the activity.

 Fumes Work in a well-ventilated area when harmful vapors may be involved. Avoid inhaling vapors directly. Test an odor only when directed to do so by your teacher, and use a wafting motion to direct the vapor toward your nose.

 Sharp Object Scissors, scalpels, knives, needles, pins, and tacks can cut your skin. Always direct a sharp edge or point away from yourself and others.

 Animal Safety Treat live or preserved animals or animal parts with care to avoid harming the animals or yourself. Wash your hands when you are finished with the activity.

 Plant Safety Handle plants only as directed by your teacher. If you are allergic to certain plants, tell your teacher; do not do an activity involving those plants. Avoid touching harmful plants such as poison ivy. Wash your hands when you are finished with the activity.

 Electric Shock To avoid electric shock, never use electrical equipment around water, when the equipment is wet, or when your hands are wet. Be sure cords are untangled and cannot trip anyone. Unplug equipment not in use.

 Physical Safety When an experiment involves physical activity, avoid injuring yourself or others. Alert your teacher if there is any reason you should not participate.

 Disposal Dispose of chemicals and other laboratory materials safely. Follow the instructions from your teacher.

 Hand Washing Wash your hands thoroughly when finished with an activity. Use soap and warm water. Rinse well.

 General Safety Awareness When this symbol appears, follow the instructions provided. When you are asked to develop your own procedure in a lab, have your teacher approve your plan.

Using a Laboratory Balance

The laboratory balance is an important tool in scientific investigations. Different kinds of balances are used in the laboratory to determine the masses and weights of objects. You can use a triple-beam balance to determine the masses of materials that you study or experiment with in the laboratory. An electronic balance, unlike a triple-beam balance, is used to measure the weights of materials.

The triple-beam balance that you may use in your science class is probably similar to the balance depicted in this Appendix. To use the balance properly, you should learn the name, location, and function of each part of the balance.

Triple-Beam Balance

The triple-beam balance is a single-pan balance with three beams calibrated in grams. The back, or 100-gram, beam is divided into ten units of 10 grams each. The middle, or 500-gram, beam is divided into five units of 100 grams each. The front, or 10-gram, beam is divided into ten units of 1 gram each. Each gram on the front beam is further divided into units of 0.1 gram.

Apply Concepts What is the greatest mass you could find with the triple-beam balance in the picture?

....

Calculate What is the mass of the apple in the picture?

....

The following procedure can be used to find the mass of an object with a triple-beam balance:

1. Place the object on the pan.

2. Move the rider on the middle beam notch by notch until the horizontal pointer on the right drops below zero. Move the rider back one notch.

3. Move the rider on the back beam notch by notch until the pointer again drops below zero. Move the rider back one notch.

4. Slowly slide the rider along the front beam until the pointer stops at the zero point.

5. The mass of the object is equal to the sum of the readings on the three beams.

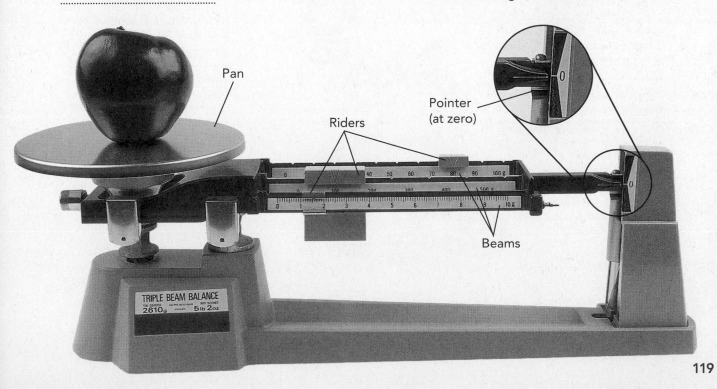

Pan

Riders

Pointer (at zero)

Beams

TRIPLE BEAM BALANCE
700 SERIES   811 SERIES
2610 g   5 lb 2 oz

Using a Microscope

The microscope is an essential tool in the study of life science. It allows you to see things that are too small to be seen with the unaided eye.

You will probably use a compound microscope like the one you see here. The compound microscope has more than one lens that magnifies the object you view.

Typically, a compound microscope has one lens in the eyepiece (the part you look through). The eyepiece lens usually magnifies 10×. Any object you view through this lens will appear 10 times larger than it is.

A compound microscope may contain two or three other lenses called objective lenses. They are called the low-power and high-power objective lenses. The low-power objective lens usually magnifies 10×. The high-power objective lenses usually magnify 40× and 100×.

To calculate the total magnification with which you are viewing an object, multiply the magnification of the eyepiece lens by the magnification of the objective lens you are using. For example, the eyepiece's magnification of 10× multiplied by the low-power objective's magnification of 10× equals a total magnification of 100×.

Use the photo of the compound microscope to become familiar with the parts of the microscope and their functions.

The Parts of a Microscope

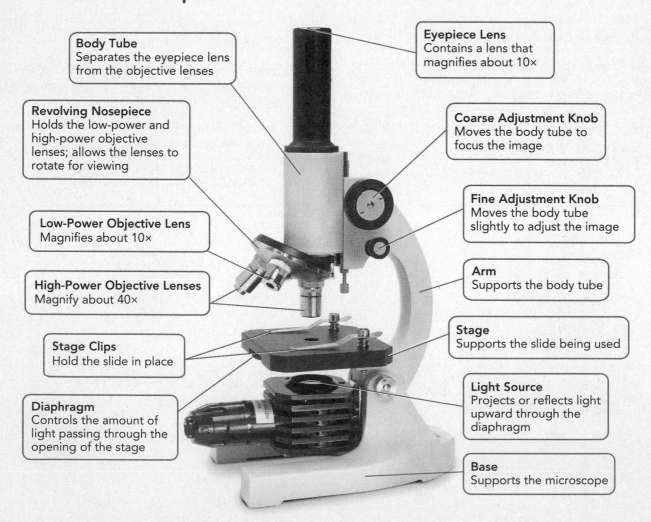

Body Tube
Separates the eyepiece lens from the objective lenses

Revolving Nosepiece
Holds the low-power and high-power objective lenses; allows the lenses to rotate for viewing

Low-Power Objective Lens
Magnifies about 10×

High-Power Objective Lenses
Magnify about 40×

Stage Clips
Hold the slide in place

Diaphragm
Controls the amount of light passing through the opening of the stage

Eyepiece Lens
Contains a lens that magnifies about 10×

Coarse Adjustment Knob
Moves the body tube to focus the image

Fine Adjustment Knob
Moves the body tube slightly to adjust the image

Arm
Supports the body tube

Stage
Supports the slide being used

Light Source
Projects or reflects light upward through the diaphragm

Base
Supports the microscope

Using the Microscope

Use the following procedures when you are working with a microscope.

1. To carry the microscope, grasp the microscope's arm with one hand. Place your other hand under the base.

2. Place the microscope on a table with the arm toward you.

3. Turn the coarse adjustment knob to raise the body tube.

4. Revolve the nosepiece until the low-power objective lens clicks into place.

5. Adjust the diaphragm. While looking through the eyepiece, adjust the mirror until you see a bright white circle of light. **CAUTION:** Never use direct sunlight as a light source.

6. Place a slide on the stage. Center the specimen over the opening on the stage. Use the stage clips to hold the slide in place. **CAUTION:** Glass slides are fragile.

7. Look at the stage from the side. Carefully turn the coarse adjustment knob to lower the body tube until the low-power objective almost touches the slide.

8. Looking through the eyepiece, very slowly turn the coarse adjustment knob until the specimen comes into focus.

9. To switch to the high-power objective lens, look at the microscope from the side. Carefully revolve the nosepiece until the high-power objective lens clicks into place. Make sure the lens does not hit the slide.

10. Looking through the eyepiece, turn the fine adjustment knob until the specimen comes into focus.

Making a Wet-Mount Slide

Use the following procedures to make a wet-mount slide of a specimen.

1. Obtain a clean microscope slide and a coverslip. **CAUTION:** Glass slides and coverslips are fragile.

2. Place the specimen on the center of the slide. The specimen must be thin enough for light to pass through it.

3. Using a plastic dropper, place a drop of water on the specimen.

4. Gently place one edge of the coverslip against the slide so that it touches the edge of the water drop at a 45° angle. Slowly lower the coverslip over the specimen. If you see air bubbles trapped beneath the coverslip, tap the coverslip gently with the eraser end of a pencil.

5. Remove any excess water at the edge of the coverslip with a paper towel.

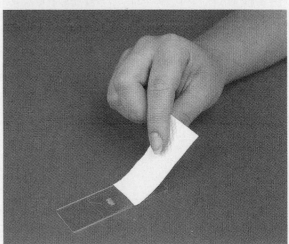

Periodic Table of Elements

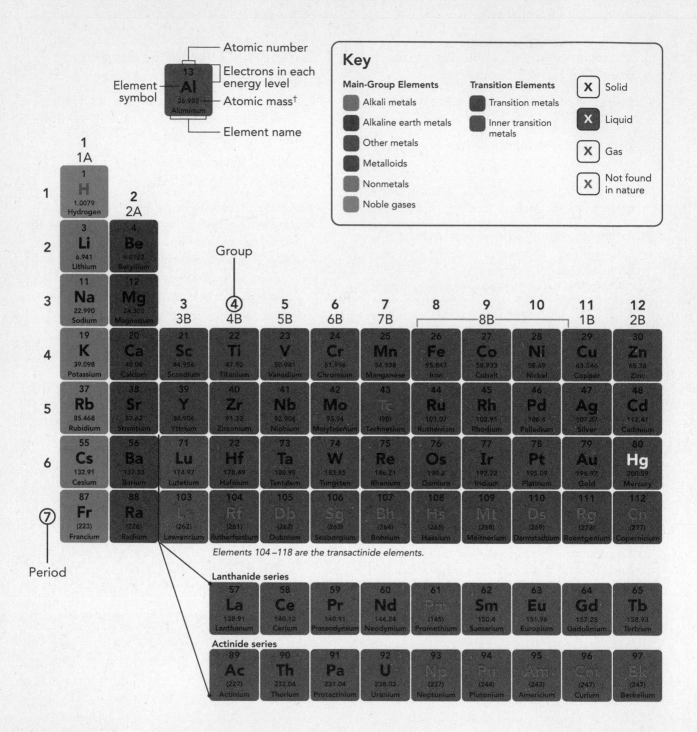

Elements 104–118 are the transactinide elements.

†The atomic masses in parentheses are the mass numbers of the longest-lived isotope of elements for which a standard atomic mass cannot be defined.

13 3A	14 4A	15 5A	16 6A	17 7A	18 8A
					2 **He** 4.0026 Helium
5 **B** 10.81 Boron	6 **C** 12.011 Carbon	7 **N** 14.007 Nitrogen	8 **O** 15.999 Oxygen	9 **F** 18.998 Fluorine	10 **Ne** 20.179 Neon
13 **Al** 26.982 Aluminum	14 **Si** 28.086 Silicon	15 **P** 30.974 Phosphorus	16 **S** 32.06 Sulfur	17 **Cl** 35.453 Chlorine	18 **Ar** 39.948 Argon
31 **Ga** 69.72 Gallium	32 **Ge** 72.59 Germanium	33 **As** 74.922 Arsenic	34 **Se** 78.96 Selenium	35 **Br** 79.904 Bromine	36 **Kr** 83.80 Krypton
49 **In** 114.82 Indium	50 **Sn** 118.69 Tin	51 **Sb** 121.75 Antimony	52 **Te** 127.60 Tellurium	53 **I** 126.90 Iodine	54 **Xe** 131.30 Xenon
81 **Tl** 204.37 Thallium	82 **Pb** 207.2 Lead	83 **Bi** 208.98 Bismuth	84 **Po** (209) Polonium	85 **At** (210) Astatine	86 **Rn** (222) Radon
113 **Nh** (284) Nihonium	114 **Fl** (289) Flerovium	115 **Mc** (288) Moscovium	116 **Lv** (292) Livermorium	117 **Ts** (294) Tennessine	118 **Og** (294) Oganesson

66 **Dy** 162.50 Dysprosium	67 **Ho** 164.93 Holmium	68 **Er** 167.26 Erbium	69 **Tm** 168.93 Thulium	70 **Yb** 173.04 Ytterbium
98 **Cf** (251) Californium	99 **Es** (252) Einsteinium	100 **Fm** (257) Fermium	101 **Md** (258) Mendelevium	102 **No** (259) Nobelium

GLOSSARY

A

absorption The transfer of energy from a wave to a material that it encounters. (17)

amplitude The height of a transverse wave from the center to a crest or trough. (6)

analog signal A signal that allows for a continuous record of some kind of action. (80)

B

bandwidth The amount of information that can be transmitted in bits per second. (95)

C

concave A mirror with a surface that curves inward or a lens that is thinner at the center than at the edges. (50)

convex A mirror that curves outward or lens that is thicker in the center than at the edges. (49)

D

decibel The number of deaths per 1,000 individuals in a certain period of time. (30)

diffraction The bending or spreading of waves as they move around a barrier or pass through an opening. (17)

diffuse reflection Reflection that occurs when parallel light rays hit an uneven surface and all reflect at different angles. (48)

digital signal A signal that allows for a record of numerical values of an action at a set of continuous time intervals. (80)

Doppler effect The change in frequency of a wave as its source moves in relation to an observer. (32)

E

electrical circuit A complete, unbroken path through which electric charges can flow. (67)

electromagnetic radiation The energy transferred through space by electromagnetic waves. (5)

electromagnetic signal Information that is sent as a pattern of electromagnetic waves, such as visible light, microwaves, and radio waves. (79)

electromagnetic spectrum The complete range of electromagnetic waves placed in order of increasing frequency. (39)

electromagnetic wave A wave that can transfer electric and magnetic energy through the vacuum of space. (35)

electronic signal Information that is sent as a pattern in a controlled flow of current through a circuit. (78)

F

focal point The point at which light rays parallel to the optical axis meet, after being reflected (or refracted) by a mirror (or lens). (49)

frequency The number of complete waves that pass a given point in a certain amount of time. (8)

G

gamma rays Electromagnetic waves with the shortest wavelengths and highest frequencies. (41)

I

information technology Computer and telecommunication hardware and software that store, transmit, receive, and manipulate information. (89)

infrared rays Electromagnetic waves with shorter wavelengths and higher frequencies than microwaves. (40)

intensity The amount of energy per second carried through a unit area by a wave. (29)

interference The interaction between waves that meet. (18)

L

longitudinal wave A wave that moves the medium in a direction parallel to the direction in which the wave travels. (7)

loudness The perception of the energy of a sound. (29)

M

mechanical wave A wave that requires a medium through which to travel. (5)

medium The material through which a wave travels. (5)

microwaves Electromagnetic waves that have shorter wavelengths and higher frequencies than radio waves. (40)

N

noise Random signals from the environment that can alter the output of a signal. (94)

O

Ohm's law The law that staes that resistance in a circuit is equal to voltage divided by current. (70)

opaque A type of material that reflects or absorbs all of the light that strikes it. (45)

P

parallel circuit An electric circuit in which different parts of the circuit are on separate branches. (72)

pitch A description of how a sound is perceived as high or low. (31)

pixel A small, uniform shape that is combined with other pixels to make a larger image. (84)

R

radio waves Electromagnetic waves with the longest wavelengths and lowest frequencies. (39)

reflection The bouncing back of an object or a wave when it hits a surface through which it cannot pass. (15)

refraction The bending of waves as they enter a new medium at an angle, caused by a change in speed. (16)

resistance The measurement of how difficult it is for charges to flow through an object. (69)

resonance The increase in the amplitude of a vibration that occurs when external vibrations match an object's natural frequency. (21)

S

series circuit An electic circuit in which all parts are connected one after another along one path. (71)

software Programs that encode, decode, and interpret information. (89)

standing wave A wave that appears to stand in one place, even though it is two waves interfering as they pass through each other. (20)

T

transluscent A type of material that scatters light as it passes through. (45)

transparent A type of material that transmits light without scattering it. (45)

transverse wave A wave that moves the medium at right angles to the direction in which the wave travels. (6)

U

ultraviolet rays Electromagnetic waves with wavelengths shorter than visible light but longer than X-rays. (41)

V

visible light Electromagnetic radiation that can be seen with the unaided eye. (40)

voltage The difference in electrical potential energy per charge between two places in a circuit. (68)

W

wave A disturbance that transfers energy from place to place. (5)

wave pulse A pulse of energy that travels through an electric circuit when it is closed. (78)

wavelength The distance between two corresponding parts of a wave, such as the distance between two crests. (8)

X

X-rays Electromagnetic waves with wavelengths shorter than ultraviolet rays but longer than gamma rays. (41)

A

Absorption (waves), 17, 26
Academic Vocabulary. *See* Vocabulary, Academic
Amplitude (waves), 6
  and energy, 10
  and resonance, 21
  and wave interference, 18–20
Analog signals, 80
Angles of incidence and reflection, 15
Antinodes (waves), 20
Application of Skills. *See* **Connect It!; Math Toolbox; Model It!; Plan It!; uDemonstrate Lab; uEngineer It!**
Assessment
  Evidence-Based Assessment, 56–57, 100–101
  Review and Assess, 54–55, 98–99

B

Balances, 119
Bandwidth, 95
Batteries and voltage, 68
Bell, Alexander Graham, 78
Binary signals, 82
  and information security, 95
  and static, 94
Bytes, 82

C

Careers
  Lighting Designer, 43
Case Studies
  Sound and Light at the Ballpark, 12–13
  Super Ultra High Definition!, 86–87
Codecs, 86
Color, 43, 45–46
  and filters, 47
Communication. *See* **Signals**
Communications systems, 91–93, 97
  See also **Information technology (IT)**
Compound microscopes, 120–121
Computers. *See* **Information technology (IT)**

Concave lenses, 52
Concave mirrors, 50
Connect It!, 4, 14, 34, 44, 66, 76, 88
Constructive interference, 18
Convex lenses, 51
Convex mirrors, 49
Crosscutting Concepts
  Cause and Effect, 30, 72
  Patterns, 82, 87, 91
  Scale, Proportion, and Quantity, 4, 10, 24, 30, 66, 70
  Structure and Function, 61
  Systems and System Models, 16, 27, 50, 66, 68, 69, 72, 78, 81, 83, 87, 94, 95, 105

D

Decibel (dB), 30
Density of sound waves, 28
Destructive interference, 19
Diffraction, 17, 37
  of sound waves, 26
Diffuse reflection, 48
Digital Learning
  Assessment, 55, 99
  Interactivity, 2, 6, 8, 9, 11, 19, 20, 22, 23, 26, 29, 32, 36, 37, 41, 42, 45, 46, 47, 52, 57, 64, 71, 72, 75, 81, 83, 84, 85, 89, 90, 95, 96, 101
  Video, 2, 10, 17, 28, 37, 43, 51, 64, 70, 80, 91
  Vocabulary App, 4, 14, 24, 34, 44, 66, 76, 88
Digital music, 81
Digital signals, 80–82
  advantages, 94–95
  sampling rate, 81
  storage capacity, 82
  See also **Signals**
Doppler effect, 32

E

Electric circuits, 67–70
  and Ohm's law, 70
  parallel, 72
  series, 71
  and signals, 77–84
Electric current
  and electronic signals, 78–79
  and resistance, 69–70
Electromagnetic radiation, 5, 35
Electromagnetic signals, 79
  See also **Signals**

Electromagnetic spectrum, 39–41
  See also **Light**
Electromagnetic waves, 35–41
  models of behavior, 36–37
  spectrum, 39–41
  wavelength and frequency, 38
Electronic balances, 119
Electronic signals, 78
  See also **Signals**
Elements in periodic table, 122–123
ELF (extremely low frequency), 79
Energy
  in electrical circuits, 67
  potential, 68
  and waves, 5–7, 10
Engineering
  Impact on Society, 23
  Prototype to Product, 75
  See also **Science and Engineering Practices; uEngineer It!**
Engineering and design process, 114–117
  communicating solutions, 117
  defining problems, 114–115
  designing, testing, and evaluating solutions, 116
  developing solutions, 115
  identifying criteria and constraints, 115
  redesigning and retesting solutions, 117
  See also **Science practices**
Extraordinary Science
  Beam Me Up!, 97

F

Features. *See* **Careers; Case Studies; Extraordinary Science; uDemonstrate Lab; uEngineer It!**
Fiber optics, 79, 93
Focal point, 49
Frequency, 8
  of electromagnetic waves, 38–39
  and energy, 10
  and resonance, 21
  of sound waves, 30–32

G

Gamma rays, 39, **41**
Greatbatch, Wilson, 75

H

Hardware, IT, 89–90
Heat rays, 40

I

Information technology (IT), 89–97
 communications systems, 91–93, 97
 components of, 90
 and digital signals, 94–95
Infrared rays, 40
Inquiry Skills. *See* **Science and Engineering Practices**
Intensity (sound waves), 29
Interference (waves), 18–19
IT. *See* **Information technology (IT)**

L

Laboratory balances, 119
Labs
 uConnect, x, 62
 uDemonstrate
  Making Waves, 58–61
  Over and Out, 102–105
 uInvestigate, 4, 8, 14, 18, 24, 25, 27, 34, 40, 44, 48, 53, 66, 67, 70, 74, 76, 77, 82, 88, 94
Lenses, 51–52
Lenses (microscopes), 120
Light, 44–52
 absorption, 17
 and color, 43, 45–47
 particle model, 37
 polarized, 35
 reflection, 15, 48–50
 refraction, 16
 speed of, 9, 16
 visible, 5, 38, 40
 wave model, 36
 wave types, 5–6
Literacy Connection. *See* **Reading and Literacy Skills**
Longitudinal waves, 7
 sound waves, 25
Loudness, 29–30

M

Magnification (microscopes), 120
Materials
 and electromagnetic waves, 35

 and mechanical waves, 5, 9, 17
 and resonance, 21
Math Connection
 Analyze Relationships, 88
 Draw Comparative Inferences, 34, 76
 Reason Quantitatively, 24
 Use Proportional Relationships, 4, 66
Math Toolbox
 Applying Ohm's Law, 70
 Cryptography, 82
 Decibel Levels, 30
 Digital Data Explosion, 91
 Frequencies and Wavelengths of Light, 39
 Wave Properties, 10
Measuring
 Internet speed, 87
 loudness, 30
 resistance, 69, 70
 speed, 40
 voltage, 68
 wave energy, 10
 wave frequency, 8
 wave speed, 9
 See also **Units of measurement**
Mechanical waves, 5–6
Medium, 5
 See also **Materials**
Microscopes, 120–121
Microwaves, 5, 35, 39, **40**
Mirrors, 49–50
Model It!, 27, 37, 50, 69, 78, 94
Morse, Samuel, 77
Morse code, 77–78, 82

N

Nodes (waves), 20
Noise, 94

O

Ohm, Georg, 70
Ohm's law, 70
Opaque material, 45
Optical fibers, 79, 93

P

Pacemakers, 75
Parallel circuits, 72
Particle model of light, 37
Periodic table, 122–123

Photons, 37
Pitch (sound waves), 31
Pixels, 84
Plan It!, 16
Polarized light, 36, 37
Process Skills. *See* **Science and Engineering Practices**
Project-based Learning. *See* **Quest**

Q

Quest Check-In
 Interactivity, 11, 22, 42, 85, 96
 Lab, 53, 74
Quest Connection, 4, 14, 24, 34, 44, 66, 76, 88
Quest Findings, 57, 101
Quest Kickoff
 Design to Stop a Thief, 2
 Testing, Testing...1, 2, 3, 64
Question It!, 17, 24

R

Radar, 35, 40
Radio, 92
Radio waves, 5, **39**, 79
Radiosurgery, 41
Rainbows, 40–41
Reading and Literacy Skills
 Ask Questions, 24, 90
 Cite Textual Evidence, 88, 90, 95
 Communicate, 74, 105, 117
 Compare and Contrast, 7, 52, 79, 88, 110
 Determine Central Ideas, 46, 66, 68, 72, 79
 Draw Conclusions, 38, 41
 Evaluate Media, 44, 47
 Identify, 61
 Integrate Information, 4, 7, 14, 17
 Integrate with Visuals, 24, 32
 Interpret Visuals, 39, 78
 Provide Critique, 61
 Summarize, 21, 27, 32, 37, 69
 Summarize Text, 76, 80, 82, 84, 90
 Translate Information, 34, 38
Reading Check. *See* **Reading and Literacy Skills**
Reflection, 15
 and cameras, 23
 diffuse, 48

of light, 46, 48–50
and mirrors, 49–50
of sound, 26
Refraction, 16
Resistance, 69–70
in series and parallel circuits, 71–72
Resolution
of analog signals, 80
of televisions, 86
Resonance, 21

S

Safety symbols, 118
Sampling rate, 81
Satellites,
telecommunications, 93
Science and Engineering Practices
Analyze Properties, 87
Analyze Relationships, 88, 91
Analyze Systems, 66
Apply Concepts, 22, 42, 57, 119
Apply Mathematics, 10
Apply Scientific Reasoning, 44
Calculate, 87, 113, 119
Cause and Effect, 30, 72
Classify, 17, 50
Connect to Society, 4, 101
Construct Explanations, 13, 14, 73, 76, 87
Develop Models, 16, 27, 50, 68, 69, 72, 81, 83, 94, 95
Draw Comparative Inferences, 34, 39, 76, 82
Engage in Argument, 4
Evaluate, 11, 85, 96
Evaluate Tests, 61
Explain Phenomena, 66, 105
Hypothesize, 28
Identify Limitations, 105
Infer, 13, 19, 34
Interpret Data, 82, 91
Make Observations, 61
Patterns, 82, 87, 91
Predict, 9, 24, 69
Reason Quantitatively, 24, 30
Relate Structure and Function, 61
Use Equations, 70
Use Evidence, 14
Use Models, 78, 87, 105
Use Proportional Relationships, 4, 10, 66, 70
Use Tables, 10
Science Notebook
Make Meaning, 21, 107, 111, 115, 116

Reflect, 5, 17, 35, 45, 106, 108, 114
Write About It, 71, 107, 108, 109, 110, 111, 112, 113
Science practices, 106–114
analyzing and evaluating, 106, 111, 116–117
classifying, inferring, observing, and predicting, 106
communicating, 109, 117
controlled variables, 109
curiosity, creativity, and skepticism, 107, 115
empirical evidence, 111
ethics and bias, 107, 109, 111
experiments and investigations, 106, 108–109, 114–116
explanations, theories, and laws, 110–111
math skills and graphs, 113
measurements, 112
models and prototypes, 106, 108, 116–117
objective and inductive reasoning, 107
scientific literacy, 111
See also **Engineering and design process**
Seismographs, 80
Series circuits, 71
Signals, 77–84
analog, 80–82
binary, 82
digital, 80–82, 94–95
electromagnetic, 79
electronic, 78–79
sampling rate, 81
transmitting sound information, 83
transmitting visual information, 84, 86
Skills. *See* **Math Connection; Reading and Literacy Skills; Science and Engineering Practices**
Slides, wet-mount, 121
Software, 89
Sound waves, 24–32
absorption, 26
behavior of, 5, 25
diffraction, 17, 27
Doppler effect, 32
loudness, 29–30
pitch, 31
reflection, 26
speed, 9, 28
transmission, 26, 83
wave types, 5–7
Spectrum, electromagnetic, 39–41

Speed (waves), 9
of light waves, 9, 16
of sound waves, 28
Standard-definition resolution (SD), 86
Standing waves, 20
Stealth technology, 35
Surface waves, 7

T

Telecommunications satellites, 93
Telegraphs, 77, 78
Telephones, 92
invention and development of, 78, 97
modern, 79
and sound waves, 83
Televisions, 86, 92
Thermograms, 40
Tools
balances, 119
microscopes, 120–121
seismographs, 80
tsunameters, 5
Translucent material, 45–46
Transmission
of light, 45
of sound, 26
of waves, 6, 10, 16
Transparent material, 45–46
Transverse waves, 6
Triple-beam balances, 119
Tsunamis, 5

U

uDemonstrate Lab
Making Waves, 58–61
Over and Out, 102–105
uEngineer It!
A Life Saving Mistake, 75
Say "Cheese!," 23
UHF (ultra-high frequency), 79
Ultraviolet (UV) waves, 5, 39, **41**
Units of measurement, 112
decibel (dB), 30
hertz (Hz), 8
joule (J), 10
megabits per second (Mbps), 87
megabytes (MB), 82
ohm (Ω), 70
volt (V), 68
UV (ultraviolet) waves, 5, 39, **41**

V

Vacuum, 5
Vibration (sound waves), 31
Video resolution, 86
Video telephony, 97
Visible light, 5, 38, **40**
Vocabulary, Academic, 4, 5, 14, 16, 24, 30, 34, 36, 44, 51, 66, 69, 76, 83, 88, 89
Voltage, **68**
   and Ohm's law, 70

W

Wave model of light, 36
Wave pulse, **78**
Wavelength, **8**
Waves, electromagnetic, 34–41
Waves, mechanical, **5**–23
   interference, 18–21
   properties, 8–10
   reflection, refraction, and absorption, 15–17, 26
   speed, 9, 16, 28
   types of, 5–7
   See also **Sound waves**
Wet-mount slides, 121
Wireless signals, 79
Writing Skills. *See* **Science Notebook**

X

X-rays, 5, 38–39, **41**

CREDITS

Photographs

Photo locators denoted as follows: Top (T), Center (C), Bottom (B), Left (L), Right (R), Background (Bkgd)

Covers

Front Cover: Stocktrek Images, Inc./Alamy Stock Photo
Back Cover: LHF Graphics/Shutterstock

Front Matter

iv: Clari Massimiliano/Shutterstock; vi: Paul Melling/Alamy Stock Photo; vii: Raimundas/Shutterstock; viii: Brian J. Skerry/National Geographic/Getty Images; ix: Gary Meszaros/Science Source/Getty Images.

Topic 1

x: Paul Melling/Alamy Stock Photo; 002: Losevsky Pavel/Shutterstock; 004: Mark Leary/Getty Images; 005: NOAA; 006: Wavebreak Media Ltd./123RF; 012: imageBROKER/Jim West/Newscom; 014: Brian Maudsley/Shutterstock; 017 BCL: Science Source; 017 BCR: Kenny10/Shutterstock; 017 BL: Roberto Lo Savio/Shutterstock; 017 BR: Nublee bin Shamsu Bahar/Shutterstock; 019: Denis Gladkiy/Fotolia; 021: Sergey Nivens/Fotolia; 023 CR: Graham Oliver/123RF; 023 TR: Lionel Le Jeune/Fotolia; 025: LightField Studios/Shutterstock; 026: Lipsett Photography Group/Shutterstock; 028 B: Andrey Kuzmin/Shutterstock; 028 C: Mike Flippo/Shutterstock; 028 T: Pukach/Shutterstock; 029: Goran Djukanovic/Shutterstock; 030: Mr_sailor/iStock/Getty Images Plus; 031: Vvoennyy/123RF; 034: U.S. Navy; 039: Gaspr13/Getty Images; 040 B: Arno Vlooswijk/TService/Science Source; 040 TL: Chuck Franklin/Alamy Stock Photo; 041: Anton Petrus/Fotolia; 043 B: Andrey Armyagov/123RF; 043 TR: Blend Images/Alamy Stock Photo; 045: Sirtravelalot/Shutterstock; 046: Yellow Cat/Shutterstock; 047 B: Falk/Shutterstock; 047 C: Havoc/Shutterstock; 048 B: Anne08/Shutterstock; 048 T: Tusharkoley/Shutterstock; 049 B: Yuelan/123RF; 049 T: TLF Design/Alamy Stock Photo; 050 B: Mediaphotos/iStock/Getty Images; 050 T: Science Source; 058: Amirul Syaidi/Fotolia; 059: EpicStockMedia/Shutterstock;

Topic 2

062: Raimundas/Shutterstock; 064: Smolaw/Shutterstock; 066: Room27/Shutterstock; 070: F.G.I CO., LTD./Alamy Stock Photo; 076: imageBROKER/Alamy Stock Photo; 078: Everett Collection/Shutterstock; 079 CR: Sirtravelalot/Shuttertock; 079 TL: Monkey Business Images/Shuttertock; 079 TR: Pressmaster/Shutterstock; 084: Marcio Jose Bastos Silva/Shutterstock; 089: CSP_Elly_l/AGE Fotostock; 090: Dotshock/Shutterstock; 092 BL: Tempura/Getty Images; 092 CR: Ruslan Ivantsov/Shutterstock; 092 TCR: Gallofoto/Shutterstock; 093 CR: Asharkyu/Shutterstock; 093 R: DAVID DUCROS/SCIENCE PHOTO LIBRARY/Getty Images; 097 B: Bettmann/Getty Images; 097 T: Jacob Lund/Shutterstock; 103 TL: Doug Martin/Science Source; 103 TR: Richard Megna/Fundamental Photographs;

End Matter

106 BL: EHStockphoto/Shutterstock; 106 BLC: Philippe Plailly & Elisabeth Daynes/Science Source; 106 TCL: Cyndi Monaghan/Getty Images; 106 TL: Javier Larrea/AGE Fotostock; 107: WaterFrame/Alamy Stock Photo; 108: Africa Studio/Shutterstock; 109: Jeff Rotman/Alamy Stock Photo; 110: Grant Faint/Getty Images; 111: Ross Armstrong/Alamy Stock Photo; 112: Geoz/Alamy Stock Photo; 115: Martin Shields/Alamy Stock Photo; 116: Nicola Tree/Getty Images; 117: Regan Geeseman/NASA; 119: Pearson Education Ltd.; 120: Pearson Education Ltd.; 121 BR: Pearson Education Ltd.; 121 TR: Pearson Education Ltd.

Program graphics: ArtMari/Shutterstock; BeatWalk/Shutterstock; Irmun/Shutterstock; LHF Graphics/Shutterstock; Multigon/Shutterstock; Nikolaeva/Shutterstock; silm/Shutterstock; Undrey/Shutterstock

Take Notes

Take Notes